Companion to the
Revised Common Lectionary

1. Intercessions

Christine Odell

Companion to the Revised Common Lectionary

1. Intercessions

EPWORTH PRESS

0 7162 0517 3

*First Published 1998
by Epworth Press
20 Ivatt Way
Peterborough, PE3 7PG*

Reprinted 1998

*Typeset by Regent Typesetting, London
Printed and bound in Great Britain by
Biddles Ltd, Guildford and King's Lynn*

Contents

Preface

I was delighted to be asked by Epworth Press to write a new set of prayers to accompany a new lectionary. Writing over 180 prayers has drawn heavily on my resources of creativity, thought, time and energy and I am indebted to those who have given me necessary support over the last year.

My thanks go to :

my husband, Peter Sheasby, for his advice, encouragement and help;

my family and friends, for their interest and encouragement;

Dudley Coates, for his help with the Revised Common Lectionary;

Cyril Rodd, Gerald Burt and members of the Epworth Press Editorial Committee;

Michael Townsend, for his thorough and sympathetic reading of my first drafts and his invaluable suggestions;

and to the Ilkley Circuit of the Methodist Church for the secondary glazing of my attic study windows!

For Anna Gelasia
who likes words
and loves God.

July 1997   Christine Odell

Introduction

Ten years ago, I wrote Volume 4 of the Companion to the Lectionary series, a collection of intercessory prayers linked to the readings and themes of the lectionary of the Joint Liturgical Group, which had been adopted by the Methodist Church for the 1975 Methodist Service Book.

This book, Volume 1 of a new Companion to the Revised Common Lectionary series, is a new set of prayers linked to the readings of the Revised Common Lectionary, a three-year lectionary that has been and will be adopted by many of the major denominations, and by British Methodism from Advent Sunday 1998.

The prayers in the volume are not only new but differ in several ways from those in the earlier volumes. Firstly, this is because the RCL sets down no central theme for each Sunday. It has Matthew, Mark and Luke years, with readings from John in all three years and a number of semi-continuous readings from other books of the Bible. This has made deciding on the emphasis of each prayer a more challenging exercise. Where I could discern a link between the readings, I have used this. Where I could not, I have, on the majority of Sundays, concentrated on the Gospel reading. But often particular passages have spoken to me with an insistent voice and I have followed their prompting. The prayers were written Sunday by Sunday, rather than following any continuous themes, although I did aim at an overall balance of content and style.

Secondly, the prayers are different because in this volume they are written for a three-year lectionary, which has involved writing almost three times as many prayers. This means that they are considerably shorter than those in Volume 4, which has put certain restrictions on creativity and layout. However, this may have made them more user friendly!

Thirdly, the world itself has changed over the last ten years. Many of our concerns are still the same, but the threat of nuclear war and the strained relationship between West and East are not such dark clouds on our horizon. On the other hand, we are much more aware of the way in which humankind threatens the existence and well-being of our planet through pollution and the exploitation of natural resources, and these concerns are more fully reflected in this volume, which also contains more prayer for Christian Unity.

Fourthly, awareness of the use of language in worship has changed over the last few years. There has been much debate over inclusive language and many exciting possibilities for new ways of speaking about and to God have been opened up. I believed, however, that in a book of intercessory prayers, it was most appropriate for me to take the *via media* and to use language that is inclusive, but not intrusive. Occasionally, when using particular biblical passages, the language is not inclusive. Occasionally, some may find it intrusive. But these will be rare occasions.

In intercessory prayer, we bring to God our concerns for the world, for humanity, for the church, and for ourselves. In the name of Jesus Christ (by whose incarnation we see that God is with us in the midst of an ambiguous world), we pray that God's work of loving, healing and redeeming creation may continue. We pray in confidence. We pray with gratitude. We pray in order to ally ourselves with God's work of salvation in and for the world.

The prayers in this book contain elements of both intercession and petition. This is because in my own mind and heart I find it hard to draw a line between prayers for others and prayers for ourselves. I believe that the church is called to offer worship to God on behalf of the world, and that the 'we' in our prayers of intercession stands not only for ourselves, as individuals or as the people of God, but for all needy and suffering humankind.

Using these prayers:

Most of these prayers have responses for the congregation to make. These can be used as printed, or silences or well-known versicles and responses could be subsituted.

Many of the prayers would lend themselves to being presented by more than one reader. This is especially true of prayers with introductory passages in italics.

Written prayers are only a starting point. These prayers are to be used in whatever way a worship leader feels appropriate – to be altered, added to, used as a springboard. As a writer, I believe that written prayers are inspired – but that the use of them should be inspired as well!

Year A

God of hope,
we pray for our future;
for the future of our world, our community, our church,
for the future of ourselves and those we love.
L: God of hope:
R: **Help us walk in your light.**

God of justice, teach us your ways.
Open our eyes to exploitation and oppression.
Show us how to live justly in this complex world.
Open the minds of the leaders of the nations:
show them that justice
is the wise way that leads to peace.
L: God of hope:
R: **Help us walk in your light.**

God of peace, teach us your ways.
Open our eyes to selfishness and greed.
Show us how to live with tolerance and understanding.
Open the minds of the leaders of the nations:
show them that peace is the wise way that leads to hope.
L: God of hope:
R: **Help us walk in your light.**

God of hope, teach us your ways.
Open our eyes to see you at work in our world.
Show us what you are calling us to do.
Open our minds and make us ready for your coming.
Open our hearts to the saving love of your Son.
L: God of hope:
R: **Help us walk in your light.**

God, in Christ you came to show us your ways of justice, peace and
love. You came to bring us hope for ourselves and for the world, for
now and for ever.
We make our prayers in our Saviour's name, and in the confidence
of the hope that he brings.   **Amen.**

God of meaning and purpose,
we puzzle to understand your intentions
for humankind, for your church, for our lives.
But in your book your intentions lie unreeled, unconcealed:
your intention that new hope should spring from old experience.
your intention to save the world.

God, you rule in humility, and so we pray
that those with power and influence in our world
might fulfill your intentions,
by being just and merciful, lovers of harmony and seekers after
peace. We pray for . . .

God, you whose love is unfailingly generous; we pray
for those calling to be saved from life-destroying need;
the hungry, malnourished, homeless, dispossessed.
Help us fulfill your intentions by responding to their call.
We pray for . . .

God, you long for our health and wholeness; we pray
for those who are sick in body, mind or spirit,
and for those who struggle to understand your intentions
as they labour under heavy burdens. We pray for . . .

God, you strengthen and guide us and so we pray
for the church, here and throughout the world.
Give us not only an understanding of your intentions
but also a vision of what it is you want us to do.

God of meaning and purpose, we pray
for ourselves, that the Spirit of Christ our King
might reign within our hearts, bestowing upon us
forgiveness, peace, joy and love, life in all its fullness.

In the name of Christ who came that God's intentions might be
revealed and fulfilled.   **Amen.**

YEAR A – **Third Sunday of Advent**

Into the earthly deserts of hopelessness and sin
our God is coming with the water of healing and forgiveness.
Lives that are grey, dismal and barren
will blossom with beauty, joy and love.

The Messiah came to bring sight to the blind.
Loving God, we pray for the visually impaired.   *Silence*
And for those who are spiritually blind,
who stumble sightlessly along life's rocky path.   *Silence*
Light of the World, may they see your face.

The Messiah came to heal the lame.
Loving God, we pray for those with disabilities.   *Silence*
And for all those who struggle on their daily journeyings,
burdened by poverty and anxiety, by guilt or fear.   *Silence*
Living Way, may they walk and leap with you.

The Messiah came to cleanse the leper.
Loving God, we pray for the outcasts of today.   *Silence*
And for those who feel alone and unloved,
forgotten by a society that doesn't seem to care.   *Silence*
Friend and Saviour, may they feel your loving touch.

The Messiah came to bring hearing to the deaf.
Loving God, we pray for those with poor hearing.   *Silence*
And for all those who are deaf to your Word,
hearing only the noisy clamour of the world.   *Silence*
Word of Salvation, may they hear your call.

The Messiah came to raise the dead.
Loving God, we pray for the recently bereaved.   *Silence*
And for all those whose lives are empty and dark,
entombed by feelings of hopelessness and sorrow.   *Silence*
Victor over death, may they find new life in you.

We make our prayers joyfully in the name of him who came to bring
good news to the poor and all humankind.   **Amen.**

YEAR A – **Fourth Sunday of Advent**

He is coming
into the arms of a young girl who bravely said 'yes',
Emmanuel: **God with us;**
into a defeated people, chafing under an alien yoke,
Emmanuel: **God with us;**
into a world darkened by sin, sorrow and death,
Emmanuel: **God with us.**

We offer you a needy world, our God.
We pray for the hungry, destitute and starving,
for the lonely, loveless and aimless . . .
Help us to remember that where there is need, we find you,
Emmanuel: **God with us.**

We offer you a suffering world, our God.
We pray for the persecuted and for victims of violence,
for those sick in body, mind or at heart . . .
Help us to remember that where there is suffering we find you,
Emmanuel: **God with us.**

We offer you a sorrowful world, our God.
We pray for the bereaved and sad,
for those depressed and defeated by life . . .
Help us to remember that where there is sorrow we find you,
Emmanuel: **God with us.**

We offer you a struggling world, our God.
We pray for those struggling against evil and greed
in this world, in society, in themselves . . .
Help us to remember that where there is struggle we find you,
Emmanuel: **God with us.**

We offer ourselves to you, our God.
We pray for the courage to say 'yes' to your Holy Spirit
so that your saving love may fill and overflow your church.
Help us to remember that wherever we are we find you,
Emmanuel: **God with us.   Amen.**

God in Christ has come to share our humanity:
the vulnerability of our flesh;
the dangers of being in our world;
the limited nature of our life.
Born at one time in history, to one people;
born for all time, to all humankind.
Born that we may have new life in him.

Compassionate God, we pray for new life
for those who suffer, as did your Son;
for . . .
We ask for the strength, healing and comfort
that only your company in their pain can bring.
Lord, in your mercy: **Hear our prayer.**

Defending God, we pray for new life
for the world, sick with many evils
that threaten the lives of the young;
for . . .
We ask for good government, led by the Spirit
of the King who came as a helpless child.
Lord, in your mercy: **Hear our prayer.**

Enabling God, we pray for new life
for all who seek to follow your Son;
for . . .
We ask for the freedom and empowerment
brought by his victory over sin and death.
Lord, in your mercy: **Hear our prayer.**

God, in Christ you came to share our humanity,
to transform our human existence
into the glorious freedom
of life as your children.
God our Saviour, you came to be one with us.
We pray that we may be one with you
and live to your praise and glory.   **Amen.**

'I am a child of the powerless.
I have no rights. My treatment is harsh and unjust.
Take my hand, Father God, and lead me through.'

Father God, we pray for the victims of governments where power is wielded for its own sake and in the interests of the powerful.
We pray for . . .
God, hear your children's cry: **Give us new life in you.**

'I am a child of the poor.
I am malnourished, physically and mentally ill-grown.
Take my hand, Mother God, and lead me through.'

Mother God, we pray for those who do not have enough of the necessities of life; food, shelter, education, medicine, work.
We pray for . . .
God, hear your children's cry: **Give us new life in you.**

'I am a child of the unloving.
I am insecure, neglected and abused.
Take my hand, Brother God, and lead me through.'

Brother God, we pray for those who suffer at the hands of the unloving, the uncaring and the abusive. We pray for . . .
God, hear your children's cry: **Give us new life in you.**

'We are the children of human parents
Struggling to follow Christ in the world.
Take our lives, Holy Spirit, and lead us through.'

Loving God, we pray for ourselves, children of human parents and your children too. You know our many needs.   *Silence*
We pray for . . . May we, made new by your Son and strengthened by your Spirit, take the hands of others and help them through.
God, hear your children's cry: **Give us new life in you.**
In the name of your Son Jesus, our Brother and Saviour.   **Amen.**

YEAR A – **Sunday between 7/1 & 13/1**

Loving God, we pray in the name of Jesus Christ
your servant, whom you upheld;
your chosen one in whom you delighted;
your Son, born to be one with humankind,
baptized with us, that we might know new life in him.

We pray in the name of Jesus Christ
for all those appointed to positions of power,
that they might rule as your faithful servants
and seek to establish justice.
In your love and mercy: **Hear our prayer.**

We pray in the name of Jesus Christ
for the church, a people called by you,
that we might delight our God by loving others
and by spreading the good news of Christ to all the world.
In your love and mercy: **Hear our prayer.**

We pray in the name of Jesus Christ
for the family of humankind, existing in need,
that they might have the material things they need for life
and be given the spiritual things they need for living.
In your love and mercy: **Hear our prayer.**

We pray in the name of Jesus Christ
for ourselves, baptized into your household,
thanking you for the new life given us in Christ
and asking for the strength and comfort of your Holy Spirit
that we might live that life to the full.
Loving God, we pray especially
for those of your family who are sick, sorrowful or afraid.
We pray for . . .
In your love and mercy: **Hear our prayer.**

Loving God, we pray in the name of Jesus Christ
who came to open the eyes of the blind
and set the captives free.   **Amen.**

Listen, God is calling,
as he called his chosen people to be a light to the nations;
as he called the disciples to follow Christ, the chosen one;
listen, God is calling!

Listen to God's voice,
calling to us from the world
in the weak voice of the powerless, the desperate voice of the poor.
  Silence
Saving God, open our ears to your call: **Help us follow you.**

Listen to God's voice
calling to us in the church
in the joyous voice of worship, the challenging voice of God's
  word.   *Silence*
Saving God, open our ears to your call: **Help us follow you.**

Listen to God's voice
calling to us from within our community
in the hesitating voice of the stranger, the trembling voice of the
  fearful.   *Silence*
Saving God, open our ears to your call: **Help us follow you.**

Listen to God's voice
calling to us through those we love
in the struggling voice of the sick, the sad voice of the bereaved.
  Silence
Saving God, open our ears to your call: **Help us follow you.**

Listen to God's voice
calling to us from within ourselves
in the still, small voice of the Spirit, the wordless voice of love.
  Silence
Saving God, open our ears to your call: **Help us follow you.**

Generous God, we pray for the grace to be your faithful followers
and committed servants, in the name of Jesus Christ, who came to
serve, to seek and to save.   **Amen.**

Good news . . .
we have been entrusted with the gospel!
We have good news for all the earth.

God of truth and love,
we pray for the mission of the church:
for Christians bearing witness to the gospel
throughout the world;
in conversations with others,
through preaching and teaching,
by loving and courageous actions.
We pray for those who are persecuted for their faith
by those among whom they live, or work, or study.
We pray that the light of your gospel
may shine in dark places.

God of grace and peace
we pray for the mission of the church:
for ourselves, as we bear witness to the gospel
within our community;
in conversations with others,
through our unity with one another and with all Christians
by our loving involvement with those who need us.
We pray for the guidance and inspiration of your Holy Spirit,
giving us the right words, right attitudes,
right ways of showing our love and concern.
We pray that the light of your gospel
may shine in dark places.

Good news. . .
we have been entrusted with the gospel!
God has given us the good news of salvation
to share with all the earth.
God of power and glory,
we pray for the coming of your kingdom of love, in the name of
Jesus Christ, your Word made flesh.   **Amen.**

(Two voices could be used.)
Amazing God, your ways are not our ways.
You turn the values of the world upside down.
Your true wisdom is the folly of extravagant love.
Your true power is made perfect in weakness.

Blessed are the poor in spirit: we pray for the poor, the powerless, the weak; those who know their need of God.
Silence. The kingdom of heaven is theirs.
Blessed are the sorrowful: we pray for the bereaved, the guilt-laden, the depressed; for those saddened by stories of violence and neglect.
Silence. They shall find consolation.
Blessed are the gentle: we pray for those caring lovingly for others; those whose acts of self-giving go unsung.
Silence. They shall have the earth for their possession.
Blessed are those who hunger and thirst to see right prevail: we pray for those who work for justice and equality; those who speak out to the powerful on behalf of the powerless.
Silence. They shall be satisfied.
Blessed are those who show mercy: we pray for those with responsiblity for the lives of others; those who seek to act with compassion and understanding.
Silence. Mercy shall be shown to them.
Blessed are those whose hearts are pure: we pray for all Christians on their earthly pilgrimage; those seeking God amidst the distractions and temptations of daily life.
Silence. They shall see God.
Blessed are the peacemakers: we pray for the healers of conflicts in and between nations, communities, families; those struggling to forgive great wrongs.
Silence. They shall be called God's children.
Blessed are those who are persecuted in the cause of right:
we pray for those who, at great cost, stand up for goodness; those who witness to your way in a cynical and uncaring world.
Silence. The kingdom of heaven is theirs.
We pray in the name of Christ, the wise fool for love. **Amen.**

All-seeing God,
you know us inside out, our deepest needs and prayers.
We ask for the gift of your Holy Spirit,
to guide us into loving you more and more,
so that the words we speak and the things we do
become outward reflections of your love in our hearts.

All-seeing God,
you tell us that what really matters
in the life of the world
is not money, or power, or self-serving,
but justice, mercy and love.
We pray for all those involved in government
that they may not pay mere lip-service to high ideals
but seek diligently to serve their people with true wisdom.
We pray for . . .

All-seeing God,
you challenge your followers to go beyond
the mere outward practice of their religion;
you ask them for their very selves.
We pray for the church, that living together in love
we might be a light for the world,
a people for your praise.
We pray for . . .

All-seeing God,
you show us, in your coming alongside us in Christ,
that promises of love are not enough,
that our words must be fleshed out by our involvement in the
    world.
We pray for all those whom you ask us to serve;
the hungry, the homeless and the needy,
and those close to us who are sick or sorrowful.
We pray for . . .

In the name of him who came to give himself totally for us,
Jesus Christ, our Light and our Lord.   **Amen.**

Creator God,
you called all things into being;
you call all things into growth,
into becoming what you mean them to be.

Creator God,
we pray for a vision of your world
as you mean it to be;
    the kingdom of your love,
    the garden of your creation.
Creator God, help us to grow:
To become what you want us to be.

Creator God,
we pray for a vision of humankind
as you mean it to be;
    a family, living in harmony and love,
    brothers and sisters, choosing and sharing what is good.
Creator God, help us to grow:
To become what you want us to be.

Creator God,
we pray for a vision of the church
as you mean it to be;
    a pattern of right living for all the world,
    a holy people for your praise.
Creator God, help us to grow:
To become what you want us to be.

Creator God,
we pray for a vision of ourselves
as you mean us to be;
    mature and loving Christians,
    obedient to your word.
Creator God, help us to grow:
To become what you want us to be.

In the name of Jesus Christ, our true foundation.   **Amen.**

Holy God,
it is hard to live in a world that despises goodness,
a world that is often cynical, corrupt and vengeful,
a world that believes in shallow realities and solutions
and does not have the courage to dig deeper down.

Forgiving God,
we find it hard to forgive our friends,
and almost impossible to forgive our enemies.
It seems only natural to seek retribution.
We pray that you will give us the strength and courage
to be prepared to pay the necessary cost of forgiveness,
to accept the hurt and not to pass it on.
We pray for situations where great wrongs have been done and for
those making decisions about how to deal with them:
in our families . . .
among neighbours and friends . . .
in our workplace . . .
among members of the church . . .
in our country . . .
within and between nations . . .
Forgiving God, we pray for understanding and peace.

Atoning God,
we want to be on your side in the world,
living in faithful obedience and doing what is right.
So we pray for your help:
to know when to speak out in anger
and when to hold our tongues;
how to offer forgiveness
and how to put right the consequences of the offence;
how to show love to the unlovely
and how to accept forgiveness for our own imperfections.
Atoning God, make us one with you and with one another.

In the name of Jesus who paid the price for us.   **Amen.**

God of the present moment,
we come to you in this time of prayer
seeking your will for the world;
your will for the church
your will for our lives.   *Silence*

We find it difficult to seek you in the present moment, loving God,
to open our hearts and our minds to you right now.
Our thoughts dart hither and thither;
back into the past, regretful, longing, guilty,
forward into the future, anxious, expectant, full of good intentions.
Help us to settle down in your presence.
May we be calm and quiet like a child clinging to its mother.
   Silence

God of justice and compassion, we seek your kingdom.
Help us to work and pray for its coming into the world,
to the poor, the oppressed, the dispossessed,
those not now fed or clothed.
We pray for . . .

God of friendship and nurture, we seek your kingdom.
Help us work and pray that its life may be seen in the church
by the spiritually hungry, the lonely,
those with a desperate need to know your love.
We pray for . . .

God of bounty and love, we seek your kingdom in our lives.
Help us find you in the beauty and order of creation,
in the Christian life of community and care.
Fed by you, clothed in joy by you, surrounded by your affection,
   we will hold your hand
as we walk along the difficult paths that lead to life.
Help us to show your kingdom in our lives
that an anxious world may seek you, and find peace.   **Amen.**

God of Moses,
you call us to serve you
in obedience to your laws,
and through lives wholly given to you.
We pray for order in the world,
for justice, peace and plenty.
We pray for order in the church,
for co-operation, vision, and mutual respect.
We pray for order in our lives,
for your guidance in all that we say and do.
God of glory: **shine through our lives.**

God of Elijah,
you call us to serve you
in faithfulness to you above all else,
through lives wholly given to you.
We pray for faithfulness in the world,
that the powerful may not be corrupted.
We pray for faithfulness in the church
that we may not be distracted from our task of loving.
We pray for faithfulness in our lives,
that we may be rooted and grounded in you.
God of glory: **shine through our lives.**

God in Christ,
you came to serve us
in faithful obedience to the requirements of love,
through a life wholly given for us.
We pray for salvation for the world,
that creation may glory in you.
We pray for the church to be filled with your Spirit,
that the glory of the gospel may bring light to dark lives.
We pray for the grace to give ourselves wholly to you
that we may live to your glory, die in your praise,
and know eternal life in the light of your love.
God of glory: **shine through our lives.   Amen.**

Merciful God, we come to you in prayer
as members and representatives of fallen humanity;
subject to many temptations.
We come to you in prayer
to ask for your help;
so that filled and strengthened by your Spirit
we may follow your Son along the narrow and difficult path of love
    that leads to life.
Spirit of wisdom and courage: **Lead us out of temptation.**

The temptation to do what we know is wrong
and to justify ourselves or put the blame on others:
Spirit of wisdom and courage: **Lead us out of temptation.**

The temptation to look for the easy, popular, short-term measure
and not to try to meet the deepest and long-term needs of the earth
    and its peoples:
Spirit of wisdom and courage: **Lead us out of temptation.**

The temptation to pray to you only as a God of power
and not as a God alongside us in the vulnerability of love:
Spirit of wisdom and courage: **Lead us out of temptation.**

The temptation to compromise our moral values
and make good ends justify dishonest means:
Spirit of wisdom and courage: **Lead us out of temptation.**

Merciful God, we come to you in prayer
as members and representatives of fallen humanity;
leaders and led, powerful and powerless,
men and women, adults and children.
We come as your church, servants, in Christ, to the world,
subject to many temptations,
to ask for your help.
We pray with confidence in the name of Jesus, God made Man for
us, and in your never-failing love.   **Amen.**

God of love, we pray for our world
which so often puts faith in things that cannot save:
in armaments and strike power;
we pray for . . . *Silence*
in the acquisition of land or wealth;
we pray for . . . *Silence*
in the superiority of race or philosophy;
we pray for . . . *Silence*
God of love, help us to put our faith in you alone,
that the world may be put right with you and made new by your
    Spirit.

God of love, we pray for the church
which so often puts faith in things that cannot save:
in the outward appearance of religion
and in social respectability; *Silence*
in the giving from what we have
but not the giving of what we are; *Silence*
in rigid beliefs, correct interpretations
and a sense of belonging to the group; *Silence*
God of love, help us to put our faith in you alone,
that the church may be put right with you and made new by your
    Spirit.

God of love, we pray for ourselves
as we struggle to put our faith in your saving love:
in times of sickness, bereavement or anxiety;
we pray for . . . *Silence*
in times of doubt, confusion or depression;
we pray for . . . *Silence*
in times when we are too busy and distracted
to find space for you. *Silence*
God of love, help us to put our faith in you alone,
that we may be put right with you and made new by your Spirit.

In the name of Jesus Christ, your gracious and costly gift of love for
the world. **Amen.**

Living God,
we have turned parts of your world into a desert,
making the lives of many difficult, damaged and dry.
We have exploited the earth, polluted its waters,
grabbed selfishly at its resources and held them tight.
Living God,
show us your better way, that the desert may blossom
and the peoples of the earth know dignity and plenty.
Help us to care for and respect your creation;
to share its resources that human needs may be met.
God of grace, we thirst for you: **Give us the water of life.**

Living God,
we have turned parts of your world into a desert,
making the lives of many difficult, damaged and dry.
We have not cultivated justice, compassion, understanding,
or sought the rights of others, only of ourselves.
Living God,
show us your better way, that the desert may blossom
and the peoples of the world find self-respect and peace.
Help us to pursue a vision of your godly and just kingdom,
offering our lives to others, obedient to the law of love.
God of grace, we thirst for you: **Give us the water of life.**

Living God,
sometimes our journey with you takes us through the desert,
our lives become difficult, damaged and dry;
our bodies become sick, our hearts ache with sorrow;
we stumble over doubts, anxieties and fears.
Living God,
lead us along your better way, to the desert that blossoms,
watered by springs of joy and peace, your living water.
Help us to endure our trials trustfully and with hope
that the truth of your love may flow through our lives.
God of grace, we thirst for you: **Give us the water of life.**

In the name of him, who poured out his life for us upon the cross,
Jesus Christ, our Saviour.   **Amen.**

'I was blind to what was going on in the world. I had shut my eyes to the suffering that war and want can bring. Then I saw, on the television, the huge, pleading eyes of a tiny, hungry child. And my eyes were opened.'

We pray for those in need . . .   *Silence*
Light of the world: **open our eyes.**

'I was blind to what was going on in my own home. I hadn't wanted to notice the signs. I couldn't believe it of a member of my own family. Then I read an article in a magazine, and the penny dropped. My eyes were opened.'

We pray for those in trouble . . .   *Silence*
Light of the world: **open our eyes.**

'I was blind to what was going on in my friend's life. I had chosen not to see how frail and preoccupied he had become. I was too busy to do anything. Then he started to cry. And my eyes were opened.'

We pray for those who are ill, anxious, or sorrowful . . .   *Silence*
Light of the world: **open our eyes.**

'I was blind to what was going on in my own inner self – to my need for God and the life that Christ has to offer. I saw myself as self-sufficient, successful, having a good life. Then the black days came, and I could see no way out. Until my eyes were opened.'

We pray for those seeking God in their lives . . .   *Silence*
Light of the world: **open our eyes.**

God of truth, help us to see things as they really are, in the light of your love for each of your children, so that our prayers and our caring may be illumined by you.
In Jesus' Name   **Amen.**

'Sir, you should know that your friend lies ill.'
Creator God,
your world lies ill:
wounded by warfare: we pray for . . . (or *Silence*)
sickened by injustice: we pray for . . . (or *Silence*)
poisoned by pollution: we pray for . . . (or *Silence*)
dying from lack of food: we pray for . . . (or *Silence*)

Creator God, we pray for new life for the world:
We thank you for hearing us.

'Sir, you should know that your friend lies ill.'
Saviour God,
humankind lies ill:
wounded by sorrow: we pray for . . . (or *Silence*)
sickened by sin and fear: we pray for . . . (or *Silence*)
poisoned by illness: we pray for . . . (or *Silence*)
dying from lack of love: we pray for . . . (or *Silence*)

Saviour God, we pray for new life for humankind:
We thank you for hearing us.

'Sir, you should know that your friend lies ill.'
Life-giving God,
your people, the church, lies ill:
wounded by division: we pray for . . . (or *Silence*)
sickened by apathy: we pray for . . . (or *Silence*)
poisoned by materialism: we pray for . . . (or *Silence*)
dying from lack of faith: we pray for . . . (or *Silence*)

Life-giving God, we pray for new life for the church:
We thank you for hearing us.

In the name of Jesus Christ, the Resurrection and the Life.   **Amen.**

YEAR A – **Sixth Sunday in Lent (Palm Sunday)**

Hosanna to the Son of David: **Hosanna, save us!**

King on a donkey, come and save us
from the power that cannot humble itself to serve us
with wisdom, compassion and justice.
Hosanna to the Son of David: **Hosanna, save us!**

God in man, come and save us
from ourselves, from sinful lives turned away from you,
your love, guidance and power.
Hosanna to the Son of David: **Hosanna, save us!**

Suffering healer, come and save us
from sickness and suffering.
Heal us by your wounds, bring us to wholeness and health.
Hosanna to the Son of David: **Hosanna, save us!**

Obedient Saviour, come and save us
from the pride and disobedience
that put ourselves and our needs before all else,
destroying our relationships with others.
Hosanna to the Son of David: **Hosanna, save us!**

Betrayed friend, come and save us
from faithlessness to your way of suffering love
and from faithlessness to one another.
Hosanna to the Son of David: **Hosanna, save us!**

Silent Word, come and save us
from hypocrisy; from the religion that speaks of love
but lacks the faith to show it.
Hosanna to the Son of David: **Hosanna, save us!**

Crucified Messiah, come and save us now.
Come and save us from sin and death
that we may rise and live with you.
Hosanna to the Son of David: **Hosanna, save us!**   **Amen.**

When hope lies dead in the tomb with Jesus
and we cannot see that things can improve
for our world, our country, our church,
for our loved ones, for ourselves:
God of Life and Love: **Raise us to new life with Christ.**

When joy lies dead in the tomb with Jesus
and life seems a dreary, uphill struggle for
the needy, the sick, the depressed,
for our loved ones, for ourselves:
God of Life and Love: **Raise us to new life with Christ.**

When peace lies dead in the tomb with Jesus
and intolerance, conflict and warfare abound
between nations, races and religions,
between loved ones and within ourselves:
God of Life and Love: **Raise us to new life with Christ.**

When love lies dead in the tomb with Jesus
and the world is a harsh, uncaring place
for the hungry, the homeless, the needy,
for our loved ones, for ourselves:
God of Life and Love: **Raise us to new life with Christ.**

When faith lies dead in the tomb with Jesus
and suffering challenges belief and trust in you
for the bereaved, the fearful, the doubters,
for our loved ones, for ourselves:
God of Life and Love: **Raise us to new life with Christ.**

Eternal God, give us the grace to die with Christ – to put behind us
the things that come between you and us, and to offer ourselves
wholeheartedly in the service of your love.
God of Life and Love: **Raise us to new life with Christ.**

In the name of Christ the Victorious.   **Amen.**

Ruler of the world, we believe in you.
We long for your kingdom of justice and peace.
We believe in the common good; justice, respect for all:
We believe in human rights but all around we see the violation of
   those rights; injustice, poverty and oppression,
and we lose heart, lose hope, lose faith.
Our seeming powerlessness to change things
saps our impulse to love and care.
Loving God, we believe: **Help our unbelief.**

Saviour of the world, we believe in you.
We long for the time when creation will be made new.
We believe that in Christ you loved us to the end,
dying for us upon the cross.
We believe that in Christ your love proved indestructible,
when he rose for us on Easter Day.
We believe in your salvation but all around we see suffering and
   sin; pain, sorrow, hatred and indifference;
and we lose heart, lose hope, lose faith.
The heavy cost of loving becomes too much for us to bear.
Loving God, we believe: **Help our unbelief.**

Sustainer of the world, we believe in you.
We long for you to fill our lives with your power.
We believe that you will change us into
the people that you mean us to be.
We believe that you are the source of love and unity:
enthusiasm, peace and joy.
We believe that you long to live in us but all around we see
   frightened believers unwilling to invite you in
and we lose heart, lose hope, lose faith.
Will the message of your love ever be heard?
Loving God, we believe: **Help our unbelief.**

In the name of the Risen Lord, who revealed himself to doubting
disciples, we pray:
Loving God, we believe: **Help our unbelief.   Amen.**

'What is it you are debating as you walk?'
Companion God, we are debating the news:
the conflict in . . .
the disaster in . . .
the famine in . . .
the accident in . . .
the crime committed . . . etc.
We are debating the news,
wondering why these things have to be.
Companion God, open our eyes to see you among the suffering of
our world. Open our eyes to see Christ's risen presence wherever
love overcomes hatred, hope destroys despair, faith challenges death.
Open our lives to Christ's risen power that we may walk the way of
love with you.

'What is it you are debating as you walk?'
Companion God, we are sharing sad news
about people we know:
those who are ill . . .
those who have been bereaved . . .
those anxious about themselves or loved ones . . . etc.
We are sharing sad news,
wondering why these things have to be.
Companion God, open our eyes to see you alongside those whose
lives are burdened, painful, fearful, or sad. Open our eyes to see
Christ's risen presence comforting, encouraging, calming and
sharing their loads. Open our lives to Christ's risen power that we
may walk the way of love with you.

'What is it you are debating as you walk?'
Companion God, we are debating the good news
of Christ's life and death and resurrection,
of the undying nature of your love for us
and of your offer of life in all its fullness.
Help us to share this good news
with those with whom we walk along life's paths,
that together we may all walk with you.   **Amen.**

Good Shepherd, your sheep need protection.
So much in the world threatens to harm or destroy them.
They are oppressed, exploited, unjustly treated,
prey to conflict and violence. We pray for . . .
We ask that the world may know life in all its fullness.
In your love and mercy: **Hear our prayer.**

Good Shepherd, your sheep need good pasture.
So many in the world do not have enough to eat.
Their lives are narrowed by need as they struggle to exist.
We pray for . . .
We ask that the needy may know life in all its fullness.
In your love and mercy: **Hear our prayer.**

Good Shepherd, your sheep need healing.
So many are sick and in pain.
Incapacitated by illness, sorrow, anxiety,
their journey through life is hard. We pray for . . .
We pray that those in trouble
may know life in all its fullness.
In your love and mercy: **Hear our prayer.**

Good Shepherd, your sheep need guidance.
So often they do not know the way they should go
but stumble along blindly, not listening for your voice.
We pray for guidance for the church . . .
We pray that we may know life in all its fullness.
In your love and mercy: **Hear our prayer.**

Good Shepherd, your sheep need saving.
So often they stray from you and get lost,
needing your costly forgiveness,
needing you to risk all to fetch them back.
We pray for ourselves . . .   *Silence*
We pray that we may know life in all its fullness.
In your love and mercy: **Hear our prayer.**

In the name of the Good Shepherd who lay down his life for the
sheep.   **Amen.**

God, our guiding light
there are many decisions we have to make
along life's path:
decisions about our relationships with others;
    about what to do with our money and our time;
    about how we should use our power to vote;
    about our relationship with you.
In Christ you show us the Way.
We pray for the guidance you alone can give   *Silence*
and we pray for . . .
This is our prayer: **Help us to know and to do your will.**

God, the source of all wisdom,
there is much we need to learn
along life's path.
We need to understand other people;
    the world around us;
    our place within it;
    and to seek a meaning and purpose for our lives.
In Christ you show us the Truth.
We pray for the wisdom you alone can give   *Silence*
and we pray for . . .
This is our prayer: **Help us to know and to do your will.**

God, the giver of life,
you have promised us everlasting life
if we follow you along life's path:
    through the bad times of sickness and sorrow
    and the good times of confidence and hope;
    along the narrow way of dedication to you
    and the stony road of self-giving love.
In Christ you show us the Life.
We pray for your guidance   *Silence*
and we pray for the fullness of life you alone can give.
This is our prayer: **Help us to know and to do your will.**

We make our prayers in the name of Jesus Christ, the Way, the Truth
and the Life for all the world.   **Amen.**

YEAR A – Sixth Sunday of Easter

Creator God, we pray for the world:
your world, created by love, lit up by your glory;
our world, spoilt by selfishness and sin.
We pray for the world;
its land ravaged, its waters polluted, its resources squandered;
its people governed unjustly and oppressively;
its nations torn apart by war;
its children hungry and despairing.
Silence
Creator God, help us to obey your commands.
Fill us with your love: **that the world may see your glory.**

Saviour God, we pray for the world:
your world, where we may seek and know you;
our world, of opportunity and temptation.
We pray for:
those rulers and leaders trying to serve their people well;
communities divided by race, class or religion;
the church, witnessing to your gospel of saving love;
ourselves, on our spiritual pilgrimage through life.
Silence
Saviour God, help us to obey your commands.
Fill us with your love: **that the world may see your glory.**

Comforter God, we pray for the world:
your world, suffused with your presence;
our world, a place of vulnerability and struggle.
We pray for:
those who are ill, sorrowful or bereaved;
those who can no longer feel you in their lives;
those seeking reassurance and guidance for the future;
ourselves, that you will fill us with love, joy and peace.
Silence
Creator God, help us to obey your commands.
Fill us with your love: **that the world may see your glory.**
Amen.

YEAR A – **Seventh Sunday of Easter**

Glorious God,
we worship you
and we long for the time
when the whole earth will see your glory:
the glory of majestic love
revealed in the life and death of Christ,
his resurrection and ascension.
Glory to God: **Glory to God in the highest.**

Help us to give the earth a glimpse of your glory
    in lives of faith lit up by joy,
    transparent with your truth.
Glory to God: **Glory to God in the highest.**

Help us to give the earth a glimpse of your glory
    by caring for the needy and unjustly treated
    and putting people before things.
Glory to God: **Glory to God in the highest.**

Help us to give the earth a glimpse of your glory
    through the love we show one another
    and the love we show to others.
Glory to God: **Glory to God in the highest.**

Help us to give the earth a glimpse of your glory
    as we share the good news of Christ
    in humble, healing ways.
Glory to God: **Glory to God in the highest.**

Help us to give the earth a glimpse of your glory
    by living in the strength and light of your Spirit
    relying on you alone.
Glory to God: **Glory to God in the highest.**

Help us to give the earth a glimpse of your glory.
Make us all one that the world may believe.
We ask this in the name of Jesus Christ,
our glorious friend and Saviour.   **Amen.**

Spirit of enthusiasm, fill us with the desire for God
that transforms hearts and minds.
Come, Holy Spirit: **our lives inspire.**

Spirit of inspiration, set our words on fire
as we tell the good news of the gospel of Christ.
Come, Holy Spirit: **our lives inspire.**

Spirit of love, bind us together in unity,
that the world may see and believe.
Come, Holy Spirit: **our lives inspire.**

Spirit of freedom, cast out our life-limiting fears
that we may love with boldness.
Come, Holy Spirit: **our lives inspire.**

Spirit of peace, empty us of guilt, anxiety and despair;
and fill us with all-sufficient faith.
Come, Holy Spirit: **our lives inspire.**

Spirit of power, blow into the life of our world,
overturning values, changing stale, selfish ways.
Come, Holy Spirit: **our lives inspire.**

Spirit of comfort, when we are ill or sad,
soothe us, strengthen us, give us hope.
Come, Holy Spirit: **our lives inspire.**

Spirit of joy, turn our tears into laughter,
our frowns into smiles.
Lead us singing into the life of God's kingdom.
Come, Holy Spirit: **our lives inspire.**

In Jesus' name,   **Amen.**

Creator God, creation was conceived by you, brought to birth by
you and is continually sustained by your parental love;
in gratitude we pray for the world:
that its beauty and variety may be treasured and its riches and
    resources used responsibly and fairly;
that its rulers and leaders may seek your guidance and govern with
    justice, wisdom and compassion;
that humankind may acknowledge all that unites us and strive to
    show one another respect and understanding;
that the wonders of creation and human love may lead us to seek
    and to know you, living God.
In your love and mercy: **hear our prayer.**

Saviour God, in Christ you came to seek and to save the lost,
    to offer us new life and make us one with you;
in gratitude we pray for all humankind in its need:
for those who are lost in poverty and hunger,
    their lives a dehumanizing struggle for existence;
for those who are lost in warfare or conflict,
    their lives in the constant shadow of death;
for those who are lost in sickness or sorrow,
    their lives eaten up by anger, regret or depair;
for those who are lost in self-destructive sin,
    their lives shallow, empty, short on love.
In your love and mercy: **hear our prayer.**

Holy Spirit, you breath life and power into God's people, uniting
them in love and praise;
in gratitude we pray for the church:
asking that you will pour your many gifts upon us,
gifts of prophecy, healing, teaching, speaking,
    of faith, service, guidance and understanding.
We pray for our church here in . . .
that you will equip us to fulfill our calling .
And we pray especially for . . .
that they may know your presence with them.
In your love and mercy: **hear our prayer.**
In the name of Jesus, Son of God and Son of Man,   **Amen.**

Loving God, we pray for those governments
who put their trust in might and strength
and not in right and justice.
We pray for peoples who put their trust in leaders
who manipulate and deceive them.
We pray for the needy, the oppressed, the persecuted
who are no longer able to trust those in power.
We pray for . . .
Loving God, we ask for a world that follows the vision of your
kingdom; a world ruled with justice, wisdom and compassion.
God, our rock and salvation: **help us build our lives on you.**

Loving God, we pray for our society
which puts its trust in success and belongings
and not in goodness and love.
We pray for those who have been hurt when let down by those
they trusted; abused children, betrayed friends and lovers, broken
families.
We pray for the lonely, the unemployed, the frail, all those let down
by our society. We pray for . . .
Loving God, we ask for a society built on lasting values, a society
where we learn to respect and care and love.
God, our rock and salvation: **help us build our lives on you.**

Loving God, we pray for ourselves, for the church,
too often putting our trust in our adherence to religion
rather than living by faith in you.
We pray for those who have looked to the church
and been let down by its shortcomings.
We pray for the spiritually hungry, the guilt-ridden, the lonely and all
who long to know and trust you.
We pray for . . .
Loving God, we want to be a church that always puts you first, a
church equipped to spread the gospel of salvation.
God, our rock and salvation: **help us build our lives on you.**
Amen.

Faithful God, we pray for those whose faith is weak:
those too distracted by the busyness of life
 to listen out for your still, small voice;
those who have been so often betrayed
 that they find it hard to trust anyone, even you;
those whose childhood faith was strong
 but proves inadequate for the realities of adult life.
We pray for ourselves, that our faith may be strengthened.
Silence
Loving God: **keep us faithful and believing.**

Faithful God, we pray for those whose faith is challenged:
those facing suffering or ridicule
 as they stand up for justice, freedom or their beliefs;
those who are ill, dying or bereaved
 asking 'Why me?' of you, loving God;
those whose old beliefs are waivering
 in the light of new thinking, growing knowledge.
We pray for ourselves, that our faith may endure all things.
Silence
Loving God: **keep us faithful and believing.**

Faithful God, we pray for those who have lost their faith:
those who cannot find or feel you
 in their everyday lives;
those whose experience of suffering or evil
 has destroyed their belief in goodness;
those whose doubts and questioning
 have led them to say 'There is no God.'
We pray for ourselves, that our faith will survive dark days.
Silence
Loving God: **keep us faithful and believing.**

We thank you, God of the past, present, and future, for all those who kept faith with you until the end of their earthly lives: for their example and their encouragement.
In the name of Christ, who stayed faithful even to death on the cross, that we might know your faithfulness to us.　**Amen.**

When we forget your promises, loving God,
and live our lives as though you are not here,
relying on ourselves, forgetting your love for us,
forgetting to be thankful;
speak to us, challenge us, nudge us.
Help us to remember your promises.

When we laugh at your promises, loving God,
and live our lives in passive acceptance
of the things that happen around us,
laughing at the idea that you can change them;
surprise us, activate us, give us new vision.
Help us to take your promises seriously.

When we are possessive of your promises, loving God,
and live our lives as though they are for us alone,
hugging them to us in our innermost selves,
unwilling to share them with others;
commission us, inspire us, open us out.
Help us to tell others of your promises.

When we need the assurance of your promises, loving God,
and live our lives in darkness and despair,
overwhelmed by pain, sorrow or guilt,
needing to know your presence with us;
reassure us, comfort us, strengthen us.
Help us to experience the power of your promises.

Loving God, you have promised that you will be with us always
and everywhere.
You have promised us that we can be one with you in Jesus, if we
but trust in you.
You have promised us new and abundant life.
Help us to rely on these promises, to live by them, and to share
them with others.
In the name of Christ, your Word to us,   **Amen.**

'I am the mother crying in the desert.
I have no more food or water for my child.
God, help me!'

We remember before God:
   the hungry . . .
   the homeless . . .
   the victims of conflict or disaster . . .

'I am the prophet to whom no one listens.
I am frustrated and full of despair.
God, help me!'

We remember before God:
   our modern day political and environmental prophets . . .
   those who have no voice . . .
   the depressed and anxious . . .

'I am the woman at odds with my family;
who feels alienated from others by my belief in you.
God, help me!'

We remember before God:
   families divided by religion . . .
   Christians lonely in their faith . . .
   the church, in this secular society . . .

'I am the man who gave up everything to follow you;
but finds the way of loving painful and hard.
God, help me!'

We remember before God:
   those struggling with the Christian life . . .
   those hurt by loving . . .
   our own Christian pilgrimage . . .

Loving God, you hear us when we call you. We make our prayers in the name of our Crucified and Risen Lord.   **Amen.**

Gracious God,
we thank you for the gift of joy.
The joy that comes to those who give their lives to you,
who are thankful and trusting,
even in difficult and dark times.
Silence

But we remember the many times
when we cannot be happy:
when we are ill or in pain,
bereaved, or anxious about loved ones.
We pray for . . .
Silence

We remember before you
those for whom life is joyless:
those struggling for food or shelter,
those lonely or depressed.
We pray for . . .
Silence

We remember the situations
when following you has made us unhappy:
when you've called us to do things we don't want to do,
when the pain of loving has made us cry.
We pray for . . .
Silence

God who smiles on us,
we ask that we might have the happiness
that you alone can give.
We ask for the grace to trust you and obey you,
whatever the situation, whatever the cost.
We ask that we might come to know the eternal life
of your kingdom of joy.

In the name of Jesus Christ, your message of love and hope.   **Amen.**

Author of love, we think about:
marriages starting in joyful love and ending in sad regret;
families where members love and need each other,
   but find it hard to get on;
friendships broken by a careless word,
   a misunderstood action;
the church, so often split by petty disagreements.

And we pray:

Help, God!
You know how important our relationships are to us.
Our relationships with: our partners;
                    our family;
                    our friends;
                    our fellow church members;
                    YOU!
but we're always messing things up!
Silence
Loving God,
help us to help one another, in love;
   to be understanding, forgiving, and tolerant;
   to build one another up.

Loving God,
we pray for those whose loving is in difficulties:
   for marriages in trouble; families in conflict;
   friends who have fallen out;
   and we pray for the church, where emotions run deep
   and tiny things can cause big rifts.
Silence
Loving God,
teach your children the art of true loving;
   to recognize the needs of others and of themselves;
   to build bridges of reconciliation.
In the name of your Son, Jesus Christ, through whose life, death and
resurrection, we have come to know the depths of your love.
Amen.

Saving God, we pray for those who have heard the good news
of your forgiving and renewing love
but have not been able to take it in;
because their hearts are hardened and unreceptive, their spiritual
lives dormant, and cynicism and scepticism have pecked away their
capacity to trust and believe.   *Silence*
We pray for the opening of ears and eyes.
Saving God, sow the word of love in human hearts:
That all may reap the harvest of abundant life.

Saving God, we pray for those who have heard the good news
of your forgiving and renewing love
and have heard and responded with enthusiasm, but whose faith, not
deeply rooted in you, has withered in adversity.   *Silence*
We pray for the indwelling of your Spirit.
Saving God, sow the word of love in human hearts:
That all may reap the harvest of abundant life.

Saving God, we pray for those who have heard the good news
of your forgiving and renewing love,
who have started to grow in the faith but now have other goals in life,
wealth, success, enjoyment.   *Silence*
We pray that we may give ourselves wholeheartedly to you.
Saving God, sow the word of love in human hearts:
That all may reap the harvest of abundant life.

Saving God, we pray for those who have heard the good news
of your forgiving and renewing love
have received it with joy and continued to grow in faith.
We remember those who have died in that faith.   *Silence*
We pray that we may be faithful all the days of our lives.
Saving God, sow the word of love in human hearts:
That all may reap the harvest of abundant life.

In the name of Christ, the Sower of the seed.   **Amen.**

Let us pray to the one and true God,
the First and the Last;
who made promises to Abraham, Isaac and Jacob;
who makes promises to all the faithful;
who holds in loving hands
our future, as well as our past.

We pray for those who dread the future:
    those with progressive or chronic illness;
    those who have lost loved ones;
    those who are lonely or depressed.
In your loving mercy: **Hear our prayer.**

We pray for those looking foward to the future:
    those in new relationships;
    those starting a new life;
    those with a special event ahead.
In your loving mercy: **Hear our prayer.**

We pray for those planning for the future:
    those in government, here and abroad;
    those working with the poor and hungry;
    those seeking a vision for the church.
In your loving mercy: **Hear our prayer.**

God of past, present and future,
help us to live in thankfulness
for all that you have done for us;
help us to live in joyfulness
because of all that you are doing for us now;
help us to live in trustfulness
in all that you will do for us in times to come.
In your loving mercy: **Hear our prayer.**

In the name of Jesus Christ, who has died,
who is risen and who will come again.   **Amen.**

Listening God,
we ask for the help of your Spirit as we come to you,
for we do not know how to pray as we ought.
In your wisdom: **enlighten all who call on you.**

We pray for those who have been disappointed
by the answers given to their prayers;
who, like Jacob working for Rachel,
have prayed for one thing and received another.
In your wisdom: **enlighten all who call on you.**

We pray for those finding it hard
to know what they should pray for;
who, like Solomon, know that you will help them
but have to decide what is most needed.
In your wisdom: **enlighten all who call on you.**

We pray for those who cannot believe
that you are still listening out for them;
who are lost in the darkness of suffering
of sorrow or despair.
In your wisdom: **enlighten all who call on you.**

We pray that you will challenge and help your children
to make the time to come to you in prayer;
to be prepared to dig into their lives
to find the buried treasure of your presence.
In your wisdom: **enlighten all who call on you.**

We pray that we may not lose patience
with the slow and secret ways of the kingdom;
that we may not discard prayer in favour of action
and lose our sense of spiritual direction.
In your wisdom: **enlighten all who call on you.**

Listening God, teach us how to pray, that we and all the world may
be transformed by your love.   **Amen.**

God of strength, touch our lives and bless us.
God of grace, touch our lives and bless us.
God of love, touch our lives and bless us.

God of strength, we pray that you will bless
those whose lives are spent in struggle:
    those who stand up and speak out against injustice;
    those handicapped physically, mentally or by illness;
    those living in poverty, or beyond their means;
    those angry with you, with others, or with themselves.
Silence
God of strength, grace and love: **bless them!**

God of grace, we pray that you will bless
those whose lives are diminished by feelings of hunger:
    those who are the victims of famine or warfare;
    those driven by a selfish desire for power or wealth;
    those who long for human companionship;
    those, spiritually unsatisfied, who are looking for you.
Silence
God of strength, grace and love: **bless them!**

God of love, we pray that you will bless
those whose lives have been given to you:
    those starting out on their Christian pilgrimage;
    those who are struggling, those who feel unfed;
    those we know who are sick or sorrowful, for . . .
We thank you for those through whom
you have touched our lives and blessed us
and remember before you those who have died.
Silence
God of strength, grace and love: **bless them!**

God of strength, touch our lives and bless us.
God of grace, touch our lives and bless us.
God of love, touch our lives and bless us.
In the name of Jesus. **Amen.**

Saving God
we remember before you
nations and communities with cause to despair:
   countries at war;
   countries divided and living in conflict.
We remember before you:
   the oppressed and the persecuted;
   the poor and the needy;
   those discriminated against;
   communities where law and order,
      morality and respect, have broken down.
Saving God, we call on you.
Speak to us.
Tell us what we should do.
Give us hope.

Saving God,
we remember before you
people with cause to despair:
   those with chronic illness;
   those who have been bereaved;
   families divided and living in conflict;
   children warped or destroyed by abuse.
We remember before you:
   those with no meaning or purpose in their lives;
   those who feel worthless or unloved;
   those eaten up by guilt or regret;
   those who have lost faith
      in the power of your love to save them.
Saving God, we call on you.
Speak to us.
Tell us what we should do.
Give us hope.

Loving God, we call on you. Whenever we feel ourselves sinking
beneath the chaotic waters of despair, reach out to us, take our hands
and save us, for the sake of your Son, Jesus Christ our Lord.
Amen.

Creator, Saviour God,
your good news is for all!
You show mercy to all humankind!

God of love,
help us to tell others about you.
Give us the help of your Holy Spirit
that we may know the right things to say
and the right things to do.
We remember before you
preachers, teachers and evangelists
and pray especially for . . .
In your loving mercy: **hear our prayer.**

God of love,
lead your church into unity.
Give us the help of your Holy Spirit
that we may learn to live together
in love, trust and understanding,
so that the world might believe.
We remember before you
the churches here in . . .
and pray especially for . . .
In your loving mercy: **hear our prayer.**

God of love,
inspire us with a vision of your kingdom
of truth and justice, peace and joy.
Give us the help of your Holy Spirit
as we work and pray for its coming.
We remember before you
those working for the oppressed and needy
and pray especially for . . .
In your loving mercy: **hear our prayer.**

In the name of Jesus, Saviour of the World.   **Amen.**

Let us pray for the church;
ourselves, who, though we are many,
form one body, united with Christ
and empowered with the different gifts
allotted to each one of us by God's grace.

We pray for those with the gift of inspired utterance;
for preachers, prophets, the experienced and the wise,
for . . .
Generous God, we thank you for your gifts:
Help us to use them well.

We pray for those with the gift of administration;
for stewards, treasurers, ministers,
for . . .
Generous God, we thank you for your gifts:
Help us to use them well.

We pray for those with the gift of teaching;
for Sunday School/Junior Church, youth and housegroup leaders,
for . . .
Generous God, we thank you for your gifts:
Help us to use them well.

We pray for those with the gift of counselling;
for pastoral visitors, ministers, those who listen,
for . . .
Generous God, we thank you for your gifts:
Help us to use them well.

We pray for ourselves:
that we may give without grudging;
 lead with enthusiasm;
 and care for others cheerfully.
Generous God, we thank you for your gifts:
Help us to use them well.

In the name of Jesus, God's greatest gift of all.   **Amen.**

When our faith has become lifeless and stale
and you, God, seem remote from our daily lives:
Loving God: **call us anew;**
Steadfast Saviour: **lead us ahead;**
Life-giving Spirit: **give us strength.**

When we see so many ways we could serve you in the world
and we do not know which we should choose:
Loving God: **call us anew;**
Steadfast Saviour: **lead us ahead;**
Life-giving Spirit: **give us strength.**

When we are afraid to commit ourselves wholly to you
fearful it will cost us dear:
Loving God: **call us anew;**
Steadfast Saviour: **lead us ahead;**
Life-giving Spirit: **give us strength.**

When we face pain, suffering, loss of those we love
and the way ahead is dark:
Loving God: **call us anew;**
Steadfast Saviour: **lead us ahead;**
Life-giving Spirit: **give us strength.**

When you want us to use good to conquer evil
and we feel reluctant to forgive:
Loving God: **call us anew;**
Steadfast Saviour: **lead us ahead;**
Life-giving Spirit: **give us strength.**

Creator God, source of all goodness,
show us the people you want us to be;
show us the things you want us to do.
In the power of your Spirit,
make us the people you want us to be,
following the example of your Son
obedient to your call.   **Amen.**

'I had to speak out against the government, however risky it might be for me. I knew that what they were doing was wrong and I could not remain silent.'

Let us pray for those
called to be prophets to those in power;
called to declare God's word
in the face of injustice, oppression and cruelty:
we pray for . . .   *Silence*

'I had to speak out against the way society was going, however unpopular it made me. I could see the unhappiness that lay ahead for so many.'

Let us pray for those
called to be prophets to their own communities;
called to declare God's word
in the face of apathy, immorality and greed:
we pray for . . .   *Silence*

'I had to speak out, to tell him that what he was doing was not right. It wasn't easy, but I knew I should offer him guidance, support and love.'

Let us pray for ourselves when we are
called to be prophets to one another;
called to declare God's word,
condemning sin but loving the sinner.
Silence

All-seeing God, loving Judge of all, you promise us that if we acknowledge our sins and repent of them you will forgive us and save us. Help us in our dealings with others to speak the truth in humble love and joyfully share the good news of salvation through Jesus Christ, your Son, our Lord.   **Amen.**

Faithful God
we need your forgiveness, constantly renewing our lives
freeing us to be
a people of faith, hope and love,
made whole by your grace.

We pray for those struggling to forgive others;
   people who have had great wrongs done
   to them or to those they love.
Loving God: **help us to forgive from our hearts.**

We pray for those who cannot forgive themselves;
   people who cannot live with the knowledge
   of what they have done or said.
Loving God: **help us to forgive from our hearts.**

We pray for those in desperate need of forgiveness;
   people torn apart by guilt or regret,
   their lives in need of rebuilding.
Loving God: **help us to forgive from our hearts.**

We pray for ourselves, learning to offer forgiveness
   by absorbing hurts and not returning them;
learning to offer to all the forgiveness
   made known in Christ upon the cross.
Loving God: **help us to forgive from our hearts.**

We pray for ourselves, learning to accept forgiveness
   as we give our lives in faith, loving God, to you;
learning to accept the forgiveness offered by others
   as we live in humble love with one another.
Loving God: **help us to forgive from our hearts.**

Loving God, help us to forgive, that we may know the breadth and
length and height and depth of your forgiving love offered to us in
Christ Jesus.　　**Amen.**

Loving God, we thank you for your many gifts to us.
Sometimes we find it hard to share them with others.
Help us to overcome our possessiveness and selfishness.

Loving God,
you gave the people of Israel
quails, manna and water in the wilderness.
You give us the food and drink we need.
Help us to share what we have with the poor and hungry.
Generous God: **make us generous, too.**

Loving God,
you offered the people of Nineveh
your forgiveness and a new start in life.
You offer us forgiveness in Christ.
Help us to share that forgiveness with those who wrong us.
Generous God: **make us generous, too.**

Loving God,
like the landowner who met the needs of the workers in the
    vineyard,
even those who had come to the work late in the day,
you offer us the unconditional love we need.
Help us to share the news of your saving love with others.
Generous God: **make us generous, too.**

Loving God,
you filled the first Christians with your Holy Spirit,
uniting them in love and equipping them for the struggle.
You give us your Holy Spirit.
Help us to share together in a common life of worship and service.
Generous God: **make us generous, too.**

Loving God, we thank you for your many gifts to us, and most of all
for the gift of yourself in Jesus Christ who came to share our
humanity that we might share in the riches of your love.   **Amen.**

Wise and loving God,
you call us to live in obedience to your will
that we might have life in all its fullness.
We pray for ourselves that, inspired by your Holy Spirit,
we may give ourselves in obedience to you.
This is our prayer: **help us to know and do your will.**

We pray for those in power, who have to make difficult decisions
which will affect the lives and well-being of many.
We pray for . . .
This is our prayer: **help us to know and do your will.**

We pray for those who are the victims of warfare or poverty, who are
calling out to us for aid.
We pray for . . .
This is our prayer: **help us to know and do your will.**

We pray for those we know who are ill or anxious or bereaved, who
need to be aware of our care for them.
We pray for . . .
This is our prayer: **help us to know and do your will.**

We pray for those involved in the upbringing of children, who are
trying to show them right from wrong.
We pray for . . .
This is our prayer: **help us to know and do your will.**

We pray for the church, as we face the challenge of Christian living
in a modern society and world.
We pray for . . .
This is our prayer: **help us to know and do your will.**

Wise and loving God,
emptying yourself of all but love
you came, in Christ, to be alongside us.
May we follow his example
by being obedient to the way of love
even to death itself.   **Amen.**

God is the landowner;
we are the vineyard
that God has planted and tended.
We are the vines,
trained and pruned by God's hand
that we may bear God's fruit.

Creator God,
we pray that we may bear your fruit;
the fruit of obedience to you:
the fruit of justice, compassion and peace
that will make this world your kingdom.

We pray for the world, for . . .

Saviour God,
we pray that we may bear your fruit;
the fruit of life made new in you:
the fruit of self-giving and unconditional love
that bears witness to your message of salvation.

We pray for those finding life hard, for . . .

Indwelling God,
we pray that we may bear your fruit;
the fruit of your life in us:
the fruit of unity, faith and joy
that suffuses our life together.

We pray for the church, for . . .

Christ is the true Vine.
We are the branches.
Source of all life,
keep us growing in you
that we may bear fruit
to Christ's glory.   **Amen.**

Loving God, giver of every good gift,
we pray that we may be your grateful people.

We pray for those with power and influence;
that they may be grateful for the opportunities
their positions give them
and show their gratitude
by fulfilling their responsibilities conscientiously
and with wisdom, justice and compassion.
Our prayer is heard: **thanks be to God.**

We pray for those with money and possessions;
that they may be grateful for the security
that their money gives them
and show their gratitude
by using what they have
to enrich the lives of those who have not.
Our prayer is heard: **thanks be to God.**

We pray for those who know your saving love;
that they may be grateful for the joy and peace
that faith in you gives to them
and show their gratitude
by sharing their faith and living in love with others.
Our prayer is heard: **thanks be to God.**

We pray for ourselves, each with special gifts from you;
that we may be grateful for the unique calling
that we, as individuals, have received
and show our gratitude
by using our talents in the service of others
and to the glory of your name.
Our prayer is heard: **thanks be to God.**

We remember with gratitude all those who lived their lives as a
thank-offering to you, loving God, for all that you have done for us
in Christ.
May we follow their example, in his name.   **Amen.**

God of majesty,
your glory fills the earth and the heavens.
You are the maker of every good thing.
We worship you and offer you our praise.

We pray that we may worship you
in the things that we do:
that, turning aside from the idols
    of power, wealth and success
we may worship you by pursuing
    freedom, justice and opportunities for all.
Glorious God: **we will worship you alone.**

We pray that we may worship you
in the things that we say:
that, turning aside from the idols
    of popularity, conformity and cynicism
we may worship you by speaking
    of goodness, forgiveness and love.
Glorious God: **we will worship you alone.**

We pray that we may worship you
by being the people that you call us to be:
that, turning aside from the idols
    of appearance, cleverness and self
we may worship you by leading
    lives radiant with humble, self-giving love.
Glorious God: **we will worship you alone.**

We pray that we may worship you
in every part of our lives,
for everything belongs to you,
creating, sustaining, life-giving God.
Glorious God: **we will worship you alone.**

In the name of Jesus, who by his life, death and rising again, revealed
the true glory of God.   **Amen.**

God of Love, you know that we don't find loving easy;
it demands so much of us:
so much commitment and self-denial;
so much thought and imagination;
so much courage and faith.
God of Love: **help us to be loving.**

Help us to love you with all our hearts,
to make our relationship with you
the most important thing in our lives,
transforming all our other relationships.
We pray for those we love and know,
especially for . . .
God of Love: **help us to be loving.**

Help us to love you with all our souls,
to commit our very selves to you
in faith and trust and hope,
and to share that saving faith with others.
We pray for the mission of the church,
especially for . . .
God of Love: **help us to be loving.**

Help us to love you with all our minds,
to seek your way for our world,
your guidance for our lives,
your truths that can set humankind free.
We pray for the future of troubled areas in our world,
especially for . . .
God of Love: **help us to be loving.**

Help us to love our neighbours as ourselves,
to treat one another with respect and understanding,
as we seek to meet the deepest human needs
and work for the coming of your kingdom of love.
God of Love: **help us to be loving.**

In the name of Jesus, Teacher of love.　　**Amen.**

God whom we worship with our lives, grant us integrity.
Fill us with your Holy Spirit,
that all we say or think or do may be motivated by you.
In your loving mercy: **hear our prayer.**

God whom we worship with our lives,
we pray for those with power and influence.
We ask that the words that they speak
and the measures that they initiate
should not spring from the desire to hold on to power at all costs,
but from the wish to serve their fellow human beings
with justice, wisdom and compassion.
In your loving mercy: **hear our prayer.**

God whom we worship with our lives,
we pray for those holding positions of responsibility within the
    church.
We ask that in the exercise of their religious duties
and in meeting the demands of their busy lives
they should not lose sight of the vision of your saving love
    that first enthralled them.
In your loving mercy: **hear our prayer.**

God whom we worship with our lives,
we pray for ourselves as followers of Christ.
We ask that our beliefs might find expression
not only in words but in loving actions.
And we ask that in our relationships with others
we may learn to love for love's sake
and not for any ulterior motives of our own.
In your loving mercy: **hear our prayer.**

God whom we worship with our lives,
we offer the whole of ourselves to you; our weaknesses as well as our
strengths, our flaws as well as our virtues, in childlike trust in your
unfailing love for us, made known in Jesus Christ, your Son.
Amen.

God of past and present and future,
make us ready for Christ's coming
into the world, the church, our lives.

Christ comes in judgment.
We pray for the world, its rulers and people
that we may respond to that judgment now
by seeking peace, justice and freedom for all.
Silence
Let us be prepared for Christ the judge.

Christ comes as the Word.
We pray for the church, its leaders and people,
that we may be open to each fresh message of Christ
for our lives today.
Silence
Let us be prepared for Christ the Word.

Christ comes as Saviour.
We pray for humankind in need of rescue,
that the lost, the sorrowful and the sick
may hear the good news of Christ's saving love.
Silence
Let us be prepared for Christ the Saviour.

Christ comes at the end.
We pray, acknowledging our mortality,
that we may face death confident in Christ's unending love
for us and for all the dying, dead and bereaved.
Silence
Let us be prepared to meet Christ in death.

God of past and present and future,
make us ready for Christ's coming
into the world, the church, our lives.   **Amen.**

Creator God,
you have entrusted us with this world.
Help us to prove worthy of your trust,
and to remember that we are accountable to you
for what we do.
We think of the things that spoil your world:
   the pollution of air and water and land;
   waste, warfare, cruelty to animal and humankind.
May we work to put things right.
This is our prayer: **Help us to know and do your will.**

Saviour God,
you have entrusted us with one another.
Help us to prove worthy of your trust,
and to remember that we are accountable to you
for what we do.
We think of the things that cause suffering:
   selfishness, injustice and hatred;
   illness, hunger and bereavement.
May we show love to others.
This is our prayer: **Help us to know and do your will.**

Life-giving God,
you have entrusted us with yourself.
Help us to prove worthy of your trust,
and to remember that we are accountable to you
for what we do.
We think of the ways in which we have betrayed you:
   keeping you out of some parts of our lives;
   failing to live together in peace and unity.
May we give ourselves to you.
This is our prayer: **Help us to know and do your will.**

In the name of him who remained trustworthy to the end, that your
trustworthiness might be revealed,
Jesus Christ our Lord and Saviour.   **Amen.**

Let us pray that we may serve Christ the King
in meeting the needs of others.

'When I was hungry, you gave me food;
when thirsty, you gave me drink.'
God with us, we pray for the hungry and thirsty
of our world:
    for the victims of famine, drought, natural disaster
    and the disruption of warfare. We pray for . . .
Show us what we should do.
Your kingdom come: **your will be done.**

'When I was a stranger, you took me into your home;
when naked, you clothed me.'
God with us, we pray for those without homes
or protection from the elements:
    for refugees, the destitute, those thrown out of home,
    those living on the street. We pray for . . .
Show us what we should do.
Your kingdom come: **your will be done.**

'When I was ill, you came to my help.'
God with us, we pray for those who are ill
    for those with chronic or life-threatening conditions,
    those who are sick in mind or spirit. We pray for . . .
Show us what we should do.
Your kingdom come: **your will be done.**

'When I was in prison, you visited me.'
God with us, we pray for those who are imprisoned:
    for criminals and prisoners of conscience,
    and those imprisoned by fear or guilt. We pray for . . .
Show us what we should do.
Your kingdom come: **your will be done.**

In Jesus' name we love and serve. In Jesus' name we pray.
Amen.

Year B

– **First Sunday of Advent**

Loving Creator, sometimes, when we look at your world,
we wonder where you are.
We see warfare, injustice and oppression,
and wonder where you are.
We see hunger, homelessness and poverty,
and wonder where you are.
Loving Creator, alert us to your presence
in the lives of those struggling for a better world,
with those who are today's helpless and hopeless victims.
We pray for . . . (and/or *Silence*)
God with us, restore us: **smile on us and save us.**

Caring Saviour, sometimes, when we look at people's lives,
we wonder where you are.
We see cruelty, immorality and indifference,
and wonder where you are.
We see illness, sorrow and death,
and wonder where you are.
Caring Saviour, alert us to your presence
in the lives of those forgiven and made new by you,
with those suffering in body, mind or spirit.
We pray for . . . (and/or *Silence*)
God with us, restore us: **smile on us and save us.**

Renewing Spirit, sometimes, when we look at ourselves,
we wonder where you are.
We see division, apathy and stagnation,
and wonder where you are.
We see shallowness and lack of vision
and wonder where you are.
Renewing Spirit, alert us to your presence
in those united by love and in the service of love,
with those seeking truth and eternal life.
We pray for . . . (and/or *Silence*)
God with us, restore us: **smile on us and save us.**

In the name of Christ, who awakens us to the depths of your love for
us, and is our Healer, Friend and Saviour.   **Amen.**

'Prepare the way for the Lord!'
Come, reveal yourself within our world, Lord.
Come with your message of justice and peace:
to the poor and exploited;
to lives overshadowed by conflict.
Loving God: **Help us prepare the way for Christ.**

'Prepare the way for the Lord!'
Come, reveal yourself in our community, Lord.
Come with your friendship and concern:
to the lonely and unloved;
to lives overshadowed by suffering.
Loving God: **Help us prepare the way for Christ.**

'Prepare the way for the Lord!'
Come, reveal yourself in the church, Lord.
Come with the gift of your Holy Spirit:
to both young and old on the journey of faith;
to lives overshadowed by doubt.
Loving God: **Help us prepare the way for Christ.**

'Prepare the way for the Lord!'
Come, reveal yourself in human lives, Lord.
Come with the offering of salvation:
to the sinner and the seeker;
to lives overshadowed by emptiness.
Loving God: **Help us prepare the way for Christ.**

'Prepare the way for the Lord!'
Come, that we may know you with us in our need, Lord.
Come with all-sufficient love:
to the sick and anxious;
to lives overshadowed by sorrow.
Loving God: **Help us prepare the way for Christ.**

By our words, prayers and actions,
Loving God: **Help us prepare the way for Christ.   Amen.**

God of our past, our present and our future,
we pray for the world,
where nothing stays the same:
governments come and go;
wars are fought and peace treaties signed;
rains fall on drought-stricken lands;
the earth quakes, the rivers flood.
(We think of . . .)
We pray for the world that is always changing,
that in the midst of change,
humankind might find you, the unchanging God, at work,
and find reasons for hope and joy.

God of our past, our present and our future,
we pray for the church,
where nothing stays the same:
ways of worship come and go;
beliefs are challenged by new ways of thinking;
the Spirit constantly renews your people;
we learn to live and share with one another.
(We think of . . .)
We pray for the church that is always changing,
that in the midst of change,
humankind might see you, the unchanging God, at work,
and find reasons for hope and joy.

God of our past, our present and our future,
we pray for our lives,
where nothing stays the same:
happiness comes and goes;
we experience and learn and grow;
unexpected events alter everything;
we suffer illness and loss.
(We think of . . .)
We pray for our lives that are always changing,
that in the midst of change,
we might find you, the unchanging God, at work in us,
and find reasons for hope and joy.
In the name of Jesus, who came to change the world.   **Amen.**

'I am too young, too inexperienced.
How can I do what you ask of me?'
Loving God, we pray for those you call to do
special and important things for you
who feel inadequate
and unsure of their abilities and strength.
Gracious God, send those you call the help of your Spirit:
   that your people, like Mary, may say 'yes' to you.

'I cannot understand how what you say will happen.
I find it very hard to believe!'
Loving God, we pray for those you call to do
new and risky things for you
who want to draw back
and are unwilling to put their trust in you.
Gracious God, send those you call the help of your Spirit:
   that your people, like Mary, may say 'yes' to you.

'I am afraid of your demands, Most High.
I am afraid to hand over my life to you.'
Loving God, when you call us to do
difficult and demanding things for you
we often run away
and are not prepared to give you what you ask.
Gracious God, send those you call the help of your Spirit:
   that your people, like Mary, may say 'yes' to you.

'I am young, bewildered and afraid,
but I am the Lord's servant.
May it be as you have said.'
Loving God, call us to serve you.
Gracious God, send those you call the help of your Spirit:
   that your people, like Mary, may say 'yes' to you.

In the name of him, who, in obedience to you, emptied himself of all
but love to be born among us and bring us salvation, Jesus Christ
your Son and our Lord.   **Amen.**

Great Deliverer,
we pray for freedom:
  from poverty;
  from oppression;
  from war.
We remember before you . . .
Great Deliverer: **free your people.**

Great Deliverer,
we pray for freedom:
  from illness;
  from loneliness;
  from despair.
We remember before you . . .
Great Deliverer: **free your people.**

Great Deliverer,
we pray for freedom:
  from sin;
  from guilt;
  from anxiety.
Silence
Great Deliverer: **free your people.**

Great Deliverer,
we pray for freedom:
  from selfishness;
  from apathy;
  from fear.
Silence
Great Deliverer: **free your people.**

In the name of Christ, who took on the limitations of human life that
we might know the glorious liberty of the children of God.   **Amen.**

God's voice was heard
above the dark waters of chaos.
God spoke, and there was light.
God's voice was heard
beside the baptismal waters of the Jordan.
God spoke, and Christ's sonship was made known.
God's voice was heard
in the words of the apostles to the baptized.
God spoke and they received the gift of the Spirit.

God our Creator, we pray:
   for the dark and chaotic areas of our world;
   for peoples deluged and swept along
      by warfare, poverty and the forces of oppression.
We pray that your voice be heard
and your light be shed . . .
Silence

God our Saviour, we pray:
   for those searching for a new way of living;
   for people longing to be washed free
      from guilt and emptiness and fear.
We pray that your voice may be heard
offering them life through your Son . . .
(and we remember those who suffer and are in special need
of Christ's renewing, healing and comforting touch . . .)
Silence

God here with us, we pray:
   for a deeper faith in your saving love;
   for a deeper awareness of your presence,
      refreshing our thirsty souls
      and binding us together in love and joy and peace.
We pray that your voice may be heard
guiding, inspiring and challenging your children . . .
Silence

In the name of Christ, God's Word made flesh, the Light of the
World, the living water.   **Amen.**

Loving God, we do not belong to ourselves, but to you:
you call us by name; you say to us 'Follow me'.

You call to us in the world.
You speak to us through the voices
   of prophets, politicians and poets.
We pray for those who question our complacency
   by speaking out against injustice and oppression.
You speak to us through the voices
   of those with whom we work and play and live.
We pray for those we know whose conversations with us
   challenge us to show your love in our everyday lives.
You speak to us through the voices
   of the needy, the unwanted, the dispossessed.
We pray for the victims of greed and warfare,
who cry out to us for help.
Loving God, we do not belong to ourselves but to you.
Show us what we should do.
Speak, Lord: **your servants are listening.**

You call to us in the world.
You say to us, 'Follow me . . .'
   through a lifetime of loving and giving.
We pray for those who need our friendship:
   those who are neglected, needy, misunderstood.
You say to us, 'Follow me . . .'
   into the dark places of sin and suffering.
We pray for those who need our support:
   those who are ill, sorrowful or afraid.
You say to us, 'Follow me . . .'
   into the kingdom of light and joy and peace.
We pray for those who need to hear the message
   of the hope to be found in Christ.
Loving God, we do not belong to ourselves but to you.
Show us what we should do.
Speak, Lord: **your servants are listening.**
In the name of Jesus Christ,
our Leader, Teacher and Saviour.   **Amen.**

Jesus calls us to repentance:
   to leave behind old ways of seeing;
                old ways of thinking;
                old ways of living;
  and follow him along the
  new way of Love.

Re-creating God, we pray that the world may be led into
new ways of seeing and perceiving human life:
  we ask that humankind we may not gaze in awe
  at the trappings of wealth and power;
  but look in compassion
  at the suffering of the poor and powerless.
In your love and mercy: **hear our prayer.**

Re-creating God, we pray that humankind may be given
new ways of thinking about what is right:
  we ask that we may not thoughtlessly accept the opinions
    of those around us;
  but voyage to discover your word of truth
    for Christian living today.
In your love and mercy: **hear our prayer.**

Re-creating God, we pray that your church may be given
new ways of living, in discipleship to Christ:
  We ask that your people may not cling to the old ways
    of selfishness and fear;
  but walk boldly with the Lord of Life
    along the way of self-giving love.
In your love and mercy: **hear our prayer.**

Jesus calls us all to repentance.
Loving God, with the help of your Holy Spirit,
we will leave behind the old ways
and follow you along the new. **Amen.**

God of
we long for a world of love and understanding,
where people of different colours, creeds and cultures
live together peacefully,
respect one another,
care for one another.
We long for your kingdom
where love has full authority.
Your kingdom come: **your will be done.**

God of wisdom,
we long for a church that is truly the body of Christ,
where members with different beliefs, traditions and ideals
worship together joyfully,
build one another up,
unite in serving those in need.
We long for your kingdom
where love has full authority.
Your kingdom come: **your will be done.**

God of wisdom,
we long for a society that is just and compassionate,
where men, women and children, wealthy and poor
work together for a good future,
value one another
provide for one another.
We long for your kingdom
where love has full authority.
Your kingdom come: **your will be done.**

God of wisdom,
may human authority be exercised with love;
may human knowledge be illumined by love;
may human lives be inspired by love for you.
Your kingdom come: **your will be done.**

In the name of him who speaks to us with authority, Jesus Christ our
Teacher and our Lord.   **Amen.**

God, our healer,
   we pray for those who are sick,
      especially for . . .
   We pray for those who look after them,
      who work to heal and to alleviate suffering,
      for medical and nursing staff in hospitals and in the
      community.
   We pray for those who are full of pain and anxiety
      because someone they love is ill.
God, our healer, be with us and make us whole.
In your love and mercy: **hear our prayer.**

God, our consoler,
   we pray for those who are sorrowful,
      especially for . . .
   We pray for those who have been bereaved
      and feel overwhelmed by sadness, anger and loss.
   We pray for those whose lives are darkened
      by depression, anxiety, fear or guilt.
God, our consoler, be with us and comfort us.
In your love and mercy: **hear our prayer.**

God, our strengthener,
   we pray for those who are weary,
      especially for . . .
   We pray for those weighed down
      by chronic illness, pain or frailty.
   We pray for those exhausted
      by the demands of work or caring for others.
God, our strengthener, be with us and refresh us.
In your love and mercy: **hear our prayer.**

Loving God, we remember how in Jesus Christ you came alongside
the sick, the sorrowful and the weary and offered them healing, hope
and strength through your gospel of salvation. It is in the name of
Christ our Saviour that we make these prayers. **Amen.**

'If only you will, you can make me clean.'
God of our salvation, we come to you,
as the leper came to Jesus,
longing to be made clean:
longing for the world to be cleansed
  of warfare, oppression and greed;
longing for communities to be cleansed
  of intolerance, materialism and violence;
longing for our lives to be cleansed
  of selfishness, indifference and sin.
God of our salvation, we come to you.
We do not want to be outcasts of your kingdom.
We want to be united in love with you and one another.
If only you will, you can make us clean.

Jesus says 'I will, be clean.'
God of our salvation, we hear from you
as the leper heard from Jesus,
a promise of cleansing and wholeness.
Open our ears to the message of your gospel.
Open our lives to accept your renewing love.
Open our hearts that we may share it with others.
God of our salvation, we hear from you
that it is your will that humankind should be made clean.

*'See that you tell nobody
but go and show yourself to the priest.'*
God of our salvation, we are called to obey you
as the leper was called to obey Jesus.
Help us to remember that as the people of your kingdom,
accepted, forgiven, made whole by you,
we are called to be obedient to the rule of love,
that the world may see, believe and obey.
Help us to keep our eyes fixed on you,
to run the race to win the never-fading garland of life.

In the name of Jesus, our healer and our master.   **Amen.**

Let us bring our friends to God in prayer.
Loving God, we pray for our friends:
   old friends we know really well
      with whom we have shared a great deal;
   new friends whom we are getting to know
      as we share time and thoughts together;
   friends at church, at work or at school;
   friends who live close by and those who live far away.
Loving God, we pray for our friends
as in silence we call them to mind.   *Silence*
Companion God: **make us good friends to one another.**

Let us bring the needs of our friends to God in prayer.
Loving God, we pray for our friends:
   for those who are ill
      especially for . . .
   for those who are sorrowful
      especially for . . .
   for those who are anxious
      especially for . . .
Loving God, as his friends brought the paralysed man to Jesus, so we
bring our friends and their needs to you, asking that you will heal,
strengthen and bless them.
Companion God: **make us good friends to one another.**

Loving God, teach us the art of true friendship.
   Free us from fear,
      that we may be open and trusting with one another.
   Free us from blindness,
      that we may be sensitive to one another's needs.
   Free us from self-centredness,
      that we may truly love and care for one another.
Help us to be friends to the friendless and needy.
Companion God: **make us good friends to one another.**

Help us to say 'Yes' to others, as you have said 'Yes' to us in Christ
Jesus, in whose name we make our prayers.   **Amen.**

God has shown us a new way in Jesus.
God has made a new covenant with us,
promising us forgiveness and fullness of life,
if we but trust and obey.

God our Creator, we pray
that the peoples of the world and their leaders
may assent to your new covenant of love and life;
to new ways of living together in peace and plenty
that cannot be contained in the old schemes
of institutionalized injustice, greed and lust for power.
We pray for new ways, bringing hope for the future, for . . .
Silence
You are our God: **and we are your people.**

God our Saviour, we pray
that human beings might acknowledge their spiritual needs
and assent to your new covenant of love and life;
to new ways of understanding your compassionate generosity
that cannot be contained in the old beliefs that led
to fear and guilt, anger and despair.
We pray for those who seek your new way.
Silence
You are our God: **and we are your people.**

God our inspirer, we pray
that we, your people, might together
wholeheartedly embrace your new covenant of love and life;
your new joyful way to salvation
that cannot be found in the old tendencies of religion
to be exclusive, complacent and burdensome.
We pray for the church, that we might be united in following
your new way of self-giving love.
Silence
You are our God: **and we are your people.**

In the name of Jesus Christ, who did not come to call the virtuous but
sinners.   **Amen.**

Dazzling God, we have beheld your glory:
the glory of Moses that is the glory of your righteousness;
the glory of Elijah that is the glory of your holiness;
the glory of Jesus that is the glory of your love.

Dazzling God, we have beheld your glory;
and we pray that it may fill the world.
Shine the glory of your righteousness in the dark places
where there is injustice, poverty or hatred.
We pray for . . .

Dazzling God, we have beheld your glory;
and we pray that it may fill your church.
Shine the glory of your holiness in the dark places
where there is disunity, persecution or despair.
We pray for . . .

Dazzling God, we have beheld your glory;
and we pray that it may fill our lives,
Shine the glory of your love in the dark places
where there is illness, sorrow or fear.
We pray for . . .

Dazzling God, we have beheld your glory
and we pray for the coming of the time
when your glory shall fill the earth.   **Amen.**

God, our hope,
we pray for those who live in despair:
those caught up in the power struggles of others,
becoming the victims of warfare and persecution,
we pray for . . . (or *Silence*)
those blinded by false promises,
and now living under unjust and uncaring regimes,
we pray for . . . (or *Silence*)
Loving God, when hope is lost and faith destroyed:
Call us to repentance, renewal and trust.

God, our hope,
we pray for those who live in despair:
those caught in the poverty trap
and unable to find a way out,
we pray for . . . (or *Silence*)
those dreading the next moment, the next day
because of illness, anxiety or loss,
we pray for . . . (or *Silence*)
Loving God, when hope is lost and faith destroyed:
Call us to repentance, renewal and trust.

God, our hope,
we pray for those who live in despair:
those caught in the web of sin, guilt and fear
unable to change and escape;
Silence
ourselves, when our pilgrimage of faith
takes us through dark places of suffering and doubt.
Silence
Loving God, when hope is lost and faith destroyed:
Call us to repentance, renewal and trust.

God, our hope, through baptism you have claimed us as your own.
May we never depair, but live by faith in your promise of unfailing
love, made known to us in the life, death and resurrection of our Lord
and Brother, Jesus Christ.   **Amen.**

Let us pray for the faithful.
God, our strength and our salvation,
we remember before you
those who put their faith in you.
We pray for those whose faith is being tested
by suffering, loss, or persecution.
In your loving mercy: **Hear our prayer.**
We pray for those who lead others along the path of faith,
for ministers, teachers, parents, and for ourselves.
In your loving mercy: **Hear our prayer.**

Let us pray for those without faith.
God, our strength and our salvation,
we remember before you
those for whom faith is not a living reality.
We pray for those for whom faith has no meaning
and life no real purpose before it ends.
In your loving mercy: **Hear our prayer.**
We pray for those who have lost the faith they had,
and feel angry, bereft or betrayed.
In your loving mercy: **Hear our prayer.**

Let us pray for the gift of faith.
God, our strength and our salvation,
we confess before you
that our faith is fickle and weak.
We pray that you will steady our faith
so that we may live and love for you.
In your loving mercy: **Hear our prayer.**
We pray that you might strengthen our faith
that we may take up our cross and follow Christ.
In your loving mercy: **Hear our prayer.**

In the name of Jesus Christ, given up to death for our misdeeds and
raised to life for our justification. **Amen.**

Loving God, when will we learn your true wisdom?

We pray for the world:
    suffering because too many people believe
        that to put themselves first is the only wise way;
    suffering because too many people cannot see the need
        for justice and the alleviation of want.
We pray for leaders and rulers of nations,
for those with power and influence in our society
and for ourselves, in our daily lives and work.
God of our lives, make us wise: **make us loving.**

We pray for the church:
    struggling to cling to its essential faith in you
        in the face of modern scepticism and scorn;
    struggling to be a house and people of prayer
        amidst the claims and clamours of everyday.
We pray for the church throughout the world,
for the congregations here in . . .
and for ourselves, in our daily lives and worship.
God of our lives, make us wise: **make us loving.**

We pray for humankind:
    searching for meaning and hope in lives
        clouded by want, or suffering, or loss;
    searching for truth and the right way to live
        with you, with one another, or with themselves.
We pray for the sick . . .
    for the bereaved . . .
    for the anxious . . .
and for ourselves, in our daily lives and spiritual quest.
God of our lives, make us wise: **make us loving.**

In the name of him who came to turn the values of this world upside down and to establish the values of the Kingdom of Love, Jesus Christ, our Judge and our Cleanser.   **Amen.**

Merciful God,
the consequences of our human sin and folly
are terrible to contemplate,
but we bring them in prayer to you,
seeking salvation for the world, for humankind,
for ourselves.

We pray for our world,
devastated and destroyed by greed and lack of
foresight:
earth rendered barren;
waters made toxic;
species wiped out.
Silence
Creator God, we pray for your world.
In your mercy: **save us.**

We pray for humankind,
dehumanized and divided by selfishness and ignorance:
children weak with hunger;
women exploited and downtrodden;
men misshapen by war.
Silence
Saviour God, we pray for humankind.
In your mercy: **save us.**

We pray for ourselves,
damaged and distorted by lack of love or
understanding:
slow to trust in you;
weakened by guilt;
afraid to love wholeheartedly.
Silence
Spirit of God, we pray for ourselves.
In your mercy: **save us.**

In the name of Christ, your gift of love and salvation to all the world.
Amen.

God of our salvation, we remember at this time how our Lord Jesus Christ faced suffering and death that the glory of your love might be revealed and draw all the world to you.
And so we pray for those who face suffering.

We bring to you, compassionate God, those who are ill; perhaps dreading what the future may hold, or undergoing painful treatment, or frustrated by the limitations illness imposes;
we pray especially for . . .
God with us, in the darkness of suffering:
May the glory of your love be revealed.

We bring to you, compassionate God, those who are in need; the homeless, the hungry and malnourished, the lonely and unloved;
we pray especially for . . .
God with us, in the darkness of suffering:
May the glory of your love be revealed.

We bring to you, compassionate God, those who grieve: those who watch over the dying, the recently bereaved;
we pray especially for . . .
God with us, in the darkness of suffering:
May the glory of your love be revealed.

We bring to you, compassionate God, those needing forgiveness; some eaten up by guilt, others burdened with empty lives or unable to love; we pray especially for . . .
God with us, in the darkness of suffering:
May the glory of your love be revealed.

We bring to you, compassionate God, our own suffering:
our pain at falling short as your children;
our pain at seeing the pain of others;
our pain embraced in the name of love; and especially . . .
God with us, in the darkness of suffering:
May the glory of your love be revealed.
In the name of Jesus Christ, who, by his sufferings, has brought us wholeness and joy.   **Amen.**

Let us pray for those who feel forsaken,
  let down by those they loved and trusted.
Let us pray for them in the name of Jesus Christ,
  hailed by the excited crowd
  who later condemned him to death.
Let us pray for them in the name of the Word of Love
  crying in desolation as he died upon the cross.

Faithful God, they feel forsaken:
  the woman and her children, whose husband and father
  have left them to go to war;   *Silence*
  the bereaved man, whose friends and neighbours
  no longer know what to say to him;   *Silence*
  the teenager, whose parents
  have turned her out of her home;   *Silence*
  the parents, whose son
  has grown up to reject them and their values;   *Silence*
  the man and his children, whose wife and mother
  has left them to be with another man;   *Silence*
  the old man, once respected, whose carers
  treat him like a naughty child.   *Silence*

Faithful God, they feel forsaken:
  those whose loved ones have died,
  who feel regretful, lonely and sad;   *Silence*
  those whose faith has died,
  who can no longer find you.   *Silence*

Faithful God, come to us when we feel forsaken, when once-spoken
words of love and praise ring hollow in our memory's ears. Come to
us, with your undying word of everlasting love and hope reborn.

In the name of Christ, our crucified and risen Saviour.   **Amen.**

When people weep
  because they are oppressed,
  because they are destitute,
  because they are being destroyed by warfare,
  because all hope for the future lies dead,

Come, Risen Lord: **wipe away all tears.**

When people weep
  because they are anxious and afraid,
  because they are ill,
  because they are racked with pain,
  because someone they love has died,

Come, Risen Lord: **wipe away all tears.**

When people weep
  because they are lonely,
  because no one listens to them,
  because people have been cruel,
  because they long for death,

Come, Risen Lord: **wipe away all tears.**

When people weep
  at the sins they have committed
  at the emptiness of their lives
  at their failures in loving
  at the thought of death,

Come, Risen Lord: **wipe away all tears.**

Risen Lord, come to us, even when we cannot recognize you through our tears, and call to us, that our lives may be transformed by Easter joy.   **Amen.**

YEAR B – **Second Sunday of Easter**

'The Word of life – we have heard it.'

Word of life, teach us how to tell the good news of salvation to those searching for the message of forgiveness and the offer of a new way of living. Speak through our conversations, our witnessing, our prayers.

That humankind may be unbelieving no longer: **but believe.**

'The Word of life – we have seen it with our own eyes.'

Word of life, teach us how to show the good news of salvation to those blind to your presence in the world. Reveal yourself to them through our loving attitudes, our smiles of friendship, our willingness to stand up and be counted on issues of justice and morality.

Teach us to share the good news: **that the world may believe.**

'The Word of life – we have felt it with our own hands.'

Word of life, teach us how to make tangible the good news of salvation to those who do not know your touch. Reach out to them through our caring actions, our willing support to those in any kind of need, the warmth of our affection.

Teach us to share the good news: **that the world may believe.**

'We share in the common life with God.'

Word of life, teach us how to embody the good news of salvation by fulfilling our calling to be the Body of Christ. Unite us in love for you, for one another, for the world.

Teach us to share the good news: **that the world may believe.**

In the name of him who comes to us that God's undying love may be seen and believed, Jesus Christ our Saviour.   **Amen.**

All-knowing God,
we find it hard to understand what happens around us;
like the disciples who found it hard to understand
    that it was the risen Christ on the lakeside;
or like the people who found it hard to understand
    that it was their long-expected Messiah upon the cross.
It is hard for us to understand what happens around us
    but we pray for enlightenment,
asking that you will explain to us, your children,
    the things that we should believe, and do, and be.

We pray for the leaders of the world;
    that they may be given a deeper understanding
    of complex issues and situations
    and how they should act to serve their people.
We pray for . . .
This is our prayer: **help us to know and to do your will.**

We pray for the church;
    that we maybe given a deeper understanding
    of what it means to follow Christ in the world
    and how we should live.
We pray for . . .
This is our prayer: **help us to know and to do your will.**

We pray for humankind;
    that we may be given a deeper understanding
    of the worth and needs of every individual
    and how we may show respect and concern for them.
We pray for . . .
This is our prayer: **help us to know and to do your will.**

We pray for ourselves;
    that we may be given a deeper understanding
    of how you, loving God, are present in our lives
    and how we can show our love for you.   *Silence*
This is our prayer: **help us to know and to do your will.**
In the name of Christ, God's Word for us.   **Amen.**

'Love shows itself in action.'
Good Shepherd, we pray for those in need:
> the hungry and the homeless;
> the victims of warfare;
> the victims of disaster; and for . . .

and for all those trying to alleviate need:
> charity and relief workers;
> peacemakers;
> medical and rescue staff.

In the name of Christ, who gave his life for us:
may your love be known and shown.

'Love shows itself in action.'
Good Shepherd, we pray for those who suffer:
> the ill and the pain-ridden;
> the lonely;
> the bereaved; and for . . .

and for all those trying to alleviate suffering:
> doctors and carers;
> pastoral visitors;
> counsellors and concerned friends.

In the name of Christ, who gave his life for us:
may your love be known and shown.

'Love shows itself in action.'
Good Shepherd, we pray for those who are lost:
> the regretful and bitter;
> the underclass of society;
> the empty and despairing; and for . . .

and for all those trying to rescue them;
> therapists and counsellors;
> social and community workers;
> ministers and missioners.

Help us to offer those around us
forgiveness, acceptance,
and the new life of the gospel.
In the name of Christ, who gave his life for us:
may your love be known and shown.   Amen.

God of love, let your love fill our lives:
        filling our hearts with joy;
        casting out sin and fear;
        guiding our thoughts and actions;
        reaching out to all.
Silence
You are the vine, we are the branches:
may we bear the fruits of love.

God of love, let your love fill our church:
        binding us together;
        inspiring worship and service;
        giving us courage and vision;
        reaching out to all.
Silence
You are the vine, we are the branches:
may we bear the fruits of love.

God of love, let your love fill our land:
        showing respect to the individual;
        caring for the needy and sick;
        protecting the young and the old;
        reaching out to all.
Silence
You are the vine, we are the branches:
may we bear the fruits of love.

God of love, let your love fill the world:
        calling for justice;
        banishing hunger;
        destroying war;
        reaching out to all.
Silence
You are the vine, we are the branches:
may we bear the fruits of love.

In Jesus' name.   **Amen.**

'This is my commandment, that you love one another.'

Loving God, teach us, your children, how to love your world:
    how to be careful stewards of your creation
    how to be responsible for fellow human beings;
    how to show concern for justice and human rights.
Loving God, teach us how to love your world.   *Silence*

Loving God, teach us, your children, how to love humankind:
    how to share with those who have not;
    how to show respect to each individual;
    how to pray and how to serve.
Loving God, teach us how to love humankind.   *Silence*

Loving God, teach us, your children in Christ,
how to love one another:
    how to be united in our trust in you;
    how to bear one another's burdens;
    how to help one another to grow in faith.
Loving God, teach us how to love one another.   *Silence*

Loving God, teach us, your children,
how to love our neighbours:
    how to listen and show acceptance;
    how to be with them in times of trouble;
    how to let you speak and act through us.
Loving God, teach us how to love our neighbours.   *Silence*

Loving God, teach us, your children, how to love ourselves:
    how to accept your forgiveness;
    how to seek the good things you offer us;
    how to enjoy the love we receive.
Loving God, teach us how to love ourselves.   *Silence*

In the name of him who lay down his life for his friends,
Jesus Christ, our Teacher, Saviour and Lord.   **Amen.**

God, our Creator, Saviour and Sustainer, we pray to you
for all those you have called to live out their Christian commitment
in the exercise of power:
    for politicians;
    for industrialists;
    for journalists;
    for educators;
asking that they may be strengthened against the temptation to
misuse their powers and that they may remain faithful to their
calling to serve you.
In your loving mercy: **hear our prayer.**

God, our Creator, Saviour and Sustainer, we pray to you
for all those you have called to live out their Christian commitment
in the service of the church:
    for ministers and lay workers;
    for pastoral visitors and church stewards;
    for those who teach the young or lead groups;
    for each member of this congregation;
asking that they may be strengthened against the temptation to
forget the needs of the world outside and that they may remain
faithful to their calling to serve you.
In your loving mercy: **hear our prayer.**

God, our Creator, Saviour and Sustainer, we pray to you
for ourselves, a people called to live out our Christian commitment
in the service of others:
    for our caring for the frail and sick;
    for our listening to the troubled and bereaved;
    for our giving to the hungry and destitute;
    for our sharing of the good news of Christ;
asking that we may be strengthened against the temptation to use
others in the fulfilment of our own needs and that we may remain
faithful to our calling to serve you.
In your loving mercy: **hear our prayer.**

In the name of Christ, who prayed for his disciples.   **Amen.**

Loving God,
we ask for the gift of your Holy Spirit
to help us to pray as we ought.
Holy Spirit: **help us.**

We ask for the energy and vision of your Spirit
for those who are tiring in the battle against injustice and
    oppression;
for those exhausted by the struggle with poverty and hunger;
Holy Spirit: **help us.**

We ask for the hope and comfort of your Spirit
for those whose lives are overshadowed by illness or pain;
for those whose lives are darkened by sorrow.
Holy Spirit: **help us.**

We ask for the peace and joy of your Spirit
for those eaten up by guilt and anxiety;
for those whose Christian life has become hard and dry.
Holy Spirit: **help us.**

We ask for the guidance and strength of your Spirit
for those uncertain how to use their money or time;
for those tempted to do what is wrong.
Holy Spirit: **help us.**

We ask for the love and courage of your Spirit
for those reaching out to comfort the distressed;
for those reaching out to others with the Good News of Christ.
Holy Spirit: **help us.**

Loving God, we ask for the assurance of your Spirit
to know your presence with us in our daily lives:
in our relationships; in our worship; in our times of pain.
Holy Spirit: **help us.**
In Jesus' name.   **Amen.**

'*God the Father, bless us.*'
God the Creator, we pray for the world,
brought to birth by your love;
where your children
>fight and kill,
>die of hunger and disease,
>oppress and exploit one another.

We pray for . . .
God, Father, Son and Holy Spirit:
we ask for new life in you.

'*God the Son, protect us.*'
God the Saviour, we pray for humankind,
whose joys and pains you came in love to share,
and who are still in need
>of repentance and forgiveness,
>of healing and comfort,
>of faith and hope.

We pray for . . .
God, Father, Son and Holy Spirit:
we ask for new life in you.

'*God the Spirit, guide us.*'
God among us, we pray for the church,
which you created, sustained and filled with love,
asking that you will give us
>vision and courage,
>unity with one another,
>the strength to serve you in the world.

We pray for . . .
God, Father, Son and Holy Spirit:
we ask for new life in you.

'*God the Father, bless us, God the Son, protect us,*
God the Spirit, guide us, now and evermore.'   **Amen.**

God and ruler of all,
we pray for law-makers:
   that our laws may embody justice, compassion
     and respect for human rights.
We pray for law-breakers:
   for a new life for the sinner
   and compassion for the victims of crime,
   for courage for those in prison for their beliefs
   in justice, freedom, you.
Your kingdom come: **your will be done.**

God and ruler of all,
we pray for the church throughout the world:
   that our religion may be a living faith,
     the expression of our loving relationship with you,
     and not just the observance of ritual and custom.
We pray for church leaders and people,
   that your love for the world may guide
     their every word and action.
Your kingdom come: **your will be done.**

God and ruler of all,
we pray for those who influence the morals of society,
   (for politicians, media people, celebrities,
   for parents, teachers, religious leaders),
   that they may exercise their influence
     with responsibility, integrity and wisdom.
We pray to be filled with your Holy Spirit
   that through our lives
     your love and goodness might be revealed
       to the world around us.
Your kingdom come: **your will be done.**

In the name of Jesus, our Master and our liberator.   **Amen.**

What is your will for the world, Creator God?
How would you have us use its abundance?
How would you have its peoples treated and governed?
We remember before you
places and situations where your will is not being done:
    the conflict in . . .
    the hungry in . . .
    and . . .
asking that you will reveal to us
how you want us to pray for them
and what you want us to do.
We are the family of Christ: **help us to do your will.**

What is your will for the church, Teacher God?
How would you have us live as the family of Christ?
How would you have us share his Good News?
We remember before you
the ways in which we have disobeyed you:
    our disunity and our petty disagreements;
    our apathy and lack of commitment;
    our betrayal of the gospel in word and deed;
asking that you will renew us and teach us again
how we should pray
and what you want us to do.
We are the family of Christ: **help us to do your will.**

What is your will for our lives, Saviour God?
How would you have us give ourselves?
How would you have your people live together?
We remember before you
those seeking or facing big changes in their lives:
    those looking for a new job or moving to a new home;
    those who have recently become ill or been bereaved;
    those whose relationships are breaking down;
asking that you will show us and them
how we should pray and what we should say
and what you want us to do.
We are the family of Christ: **help us to do your will.   Amen.**

Loving God,
    make your world a new creation:
    sow the seeds of
            justice, wisdom and compassion,
    that we may reap the harvest of
            freedom, peace and plenty.
This is our prayer: **help us to know and to do your will.**

Loving God,
    make humankind a new creation:
    sow the seeds of
            forgiveness, healing and hope,
    that we may reap the harvest of
            renewal, wholeness and joy.
This is our prayer: **help us to know and to do your will.**

Loving God,
    make your church a new creation:
    sow the seeds of
            faith, unity and calling
    that we may reap the harvest of
            salvation for the world.
This is our prayer: **help us to know and to do your will.**

Loving God,
    make each one of us a new creation:
    sow the seeds of
            love, trust and commitment
    that we may reap the harvest of
            eternal life in you.
This is our prayer: **help us to know and to do your will.**

In the name of him in whom and with whom we are united,
Christ our Lord.   **Amen.**

Almighty God,
    we pray for those who feel small
    as they face up to giants of power,
    to uncaring employers, unjust governments,
    to the gun, the bulldozer, the torture chamber.
We pray for . . .
God of power: **defend and strengthen us.**

Almighty God,
    we pray for those who feel defenceless
    as their lives slip from their control:
    for those weak in body, mind or spirit;
    for those destitute, neglected, or abused.
We pray for . . .
God of power: **defend and strengthen us.**

Almighty God,
    we pray for those who feel helpless
    as they watch the suffering of those they love:
    the pain of physical disease;
    or the pain of failing lives and relationships.
We pray for . . .
God of power: **defend and strengthen us.**

Almighty God,
    we pray for those who feel powerless
    as storms of life threaten to engulf them:
    for those who have been bereaved;
    for those submerged in fear and despair.
We pray for . . .
God of power: **defend and strengthen us.**

In the name of him who calmed the storm and rescued his disciples,
Jesus Christ, our Saviour.   **Amen.**

Let us pray for those facing death:
    the family gathered at the bedside of a loved one;
    the friend waiting by the telephone for news;
    the young soldier going into battle;
    the mother cradling her starving child;
    the criminal on death row;
    the person with a terminal illness;
    the person contemplating suicide;
    for . . .
Eternal and loving parent of us all,
when death, its mystery and finality
becomes the overshadowing reality in our lives
be with us,
    the light in our darkness,
    the hope in our sorrow and fear.
God of life and death: **hear our prayer.**

Let us pray for those who have been bereaved:
    those too shocked to take in what has happened;
    those angry with the person who has died and with you;
    those eaten away by remorse and guilt;
    those whose world has collapsed.
We bring to you . . . their sorrow,
                their pain,
                their loneliness,
                their anxiety,
praying especially for . . .
Eternal and loving parent of us all,
when grief and desolation overwhelm us
and we can find no comfort or peace,
be with us,
    the light in our darkness,
    the hope in our sorrow and fear.
You are the giver of eternal life.
God of life and death: **hear our prayer.**
In the name of him, who gave up everything, even his own life, that
we might know the love and life that never die, Jesus Christ, our
Risen Saviour.   **Amen.**

Loving God,
we remember how you called David to be a king
and we pray for those who lead and govern the nations,
that they, too, may be wise shepherds of their sheep.
We pray for . . .
Silence
Our prayers are heard: **Thanks be to God.**

Loving God,
we remember how you called Ezekiel to be a prophet
and we pray for those who speak out against injustice and evil,
that they, too, may be full of your Spirit.
We pray for . . .
Silence
Our prayers are heard: **Thanks be to God.**

Loving God,
we remember how Jesus commissioned the apostles
and we pray for the church, doing Christ's work on earth,
that we, too, may be heralds of your kingdom.
We pray for . . .
Silence
Our prayers are heard: **Thanks be to God.**

Loving God,
we remember how you called Paul to be Christ's follower
and we pray for ourselves, also called by you,
that your power may be seen in our weakness
and our lives show that your grace is all we need.
Silence
Our prayers are heard: **Thanks be to God.**

In the name of Jesus, Son of David, the Christ, the Anointed One,
who came to call us back to you, our Creator.   **Amen.**

God of truth and love,
we long to be on your side,
and so we pray for:
    wisdom, to understand your will;
    courage, to stand up for truth and goodness;
    faith, that despite our trials, we shall not be overcome.
In your love and mercy: **hear our prayer.**

God of truth and love,
we long to be on your side in the world,
and so we pray for:
    wisdom, to have a true understanding of the world;
    courage, to stand up against injustice and greed;
    faith, that despite our trials, we shall not be overcome.
In your love and mercy: **hear our prayer.**

God of truth and love,
we long to be on your side alongside others,
and so we pray for:
    wisdom, to understand and meet the real needs of others;
    courage, to open ourselves to the pain of loving;
    faith, that despite our trials, we shall not be overcome.
In your love and mercy: **hear our prayer.**

God of truth and love,
we long to be on your side as the church,
and so we pray for:
    wisdom, to have a true understanding of your gospel;
    courage, to share its good news with those around us;
    faith, that despite our trials, we shall not be overcome.
In your love and mercy: **hear our prayer.**

In the name of him on whom we set our hope, Jesus Christ our
Judge and Saviour.   **Amen.**

'When Jesus came ashore and saw a large crowd, his heart went out to them, because they were like sheep without a shepherd.'

When we are lost, led astray by unwise and uncaring leaders or
    false promises and teaching:
Loving Shepherd of your sheep: **guide us.**
We pray for . . .   *Silence*

When we are hungry, for food, for love, or because we have
    not fed upon you in our hearts:
Loving Shepherd of your sheep: **feed us.**
We pray for . . .   *Silence*

When we are ill or injured, in body, mind or spirit:
Loving Shepherd of your sheep: **heal us.**
We pray for . . .   *Silence*

When we are sorrowful, bereft of someone we love:
Loving Shepherd of your sheep: **comfort us.**
We pray for . . .   *Silence*

When we are afraid, our lives darkened by thoughts of what we
    have to do or to endure:
Loving Shepherd of your sheep: **encourage us.**
We pray for . . .   *Silence*

We ask that, as Jesus's heart went out to the crowds that sought him,
so might our hearts also be moved towards those around us, in his
name.   **Amen.**

Let us pray to God for the world,
that its peoples may have what they need:
>> freedom;
>> justice;
>> security;
>> peace.
God our nourisher, we offer you our prayers and ourselves:
Take us, bless us, use us.

Let us pray to God for humankind,
that every man, woman and child may have what they need:
>> food;
>> shelter;
>> medicine;
>> education.
God our nourisher, we offer you our prayers and ourselves:
Take us, bless us, use us.

Let us pray to God for those who suffer,
that they may have the help they need:
>> healing;
>> comfort;
>> forgiveness;
>> hope.
God our nourisher, we offer you our prayers and ourselves:
Take us, bless us, use us.

Let us pray to God for ourselves,
that we may receive what we most need:
>> faith;
>> love;
>> strength;
>> wisdom.
God our nourisher, we offer you our prayers and ourselves:
Take us, bless us, use us.

In the name of Jesus, the Bread of Life.   **Amen.**

Let us pray for the hungry:
      for those who hunger after
          justice, freedom and peace;   *Silence*
      for those who hunger after
          food, medicine and shelter;   *Silence*
      for those who hunger after
          employment, empowerment and education.   *Silence*
Loving God, feed us: **feed us with the bread of eternal life.**

Let us pray for the hungry:
      for those who hunger after
          health and wholeness;   *Silence*
      for those who hunger after
          comfort and company;   *Silence*
      for those who hunger after
          reassurance and peace.   *Silence*
Loving God, feed us: **feed us with the bread of eternal life.**

Let us pray for the hungry:
      for those who hunger after
          forgiveness and reconciliation;   *Silence*
      for those who hunger after
          meaning and purpose;   *Silence*
      for those who hunger after
          faith and love.   *Silence*
Loving God, feed us: **feed us with the bread of eternal life.**

Jesus Christ is the bread come down from heaven
that brings life to the world.

In his name we pray for all who hunger in any way.

Loving God, feed us: **feed us with the bread of eternal life.**
Amen.

Let us pray for those who seek the good things in life.

'I work long hours to provide for myself and my family. We have a lovely house, and a very good standard of living. We lack for nothing . . . so why am I still dissatisfied?'

Bread of life, we pray for those who are materially rich yet spiritually poor. We ask that our need for you and for one another should not be forgotten in our pursuit of the things we want.

'Life is dull and grey. One day can be pretty much like another. At least drink and drugs bring colour and excitement into my existence. For a little while.'

Bread of life, we pray for those trying to escape from the emptiness and pain of their existence. We ask that we may find meaning, challenge and joy in our love for you and for one another.

'I do believe in you, God. I would like to know the peace and joy and love that only you can give. But there is so much that I have to get done, and so little time to do it!'

Bread of life, we pray for those who long for faith but are afraid to commit themselves to you. We ask that our lives may be driven by a deep hunger for you and that we may feed on you in our hearts by faith, both now and for ever.

In the name of him whose body was broken
and whose blood was shed
that we may feast in God's eternal kingdom,
Jesus Christ, our all-sufficient Saviour.   **Amen.**

All-knowing God, we pray for
all who have authority and influence over others:
   for the leaders of the nations
     and our own government;
   for the leaders of the church
     and our own ministers;
   for journalists
     and teachers;
   for youth workers
     and parents;
asking that they may exercise their responsibility
   with justice and compassion,
   with integrity and truthfulness
   with common sense and imagination.
   Silence
We ask for a heart with skill to listen:
we ask for your true wisdom.

All-knowing God, we pray for
ourselves, as we seek to obey your will for our lives:
   for the faith
     that leads to knowledge of you;
   for the love
     that leads to understanding of others;
   for the sensitivity
     that leads to helpful actions and words;
   for the humility
     that leaves our minds open to new insights;
asking that we may serve you and one another
   with heart and mind and soul,
   with prayerful words and deeds,
   with joy and enthusiasm.
   Silence
We ask for a heart with skill to listen:
we ask for your true wisdom.
In the name of him in whom we live and who lives in us,
Jesus Christ the Wise. **Amen.**

'Put on the full armour provided by God,
so that you may be able to stand firm.'

'Fasten on the belt of truth.'
Show the people of the world your truth, loving God,
that they may be set free
to live and work to your praise.

'For a breastplate, put on integrity.'
Make your people whole, loving God,
that our words, our attitudes, our deeds
may together reflect your love
towards all needy humankind.

'Let the shoes on your feet be the gospel of peace.'
Give your people a sure footing, loving God,
that we may stand secure in the knowledge of your love,
able to reach out to help and comfort those around us
caught up in conflict and anxiety.

'Take up the great shield of faith.'
Strengthen your people's faith in you, loving God,
that together we may never be overcome
by the trials and pains of life
but be a sign of hope to a suffering world.

'Accept salvation as your helmet.'
Dispel your people's fears, loving God,
that we may boldly follow Christ
along the path of saving, suffering love.

'Accept the sword which the Spirit gives you,
the word of God.'
Speak through your people, loving God,
that your church may be a faithful witness
to the new life to be found in you.
Loving God, give us the help of your Holy Spirit,
that the world may see and believe.   **Amen.**

We want to keep our hands clean, holy God.
We don't want to feel defiled by the dirt of the world.

For those with political power,
   who do not want to be tainted by contact
     with the poor and the oppressed;
for those who have enough and to spare,
   who do not want their enjoyment sullied
     by thoughts of the hungry and homeless;
for those happy in their cosy circle of family and friends
   who do not want that circle pulled out of shape
     by reaching out to the lonely and outcast;
we pray:
Spirit of God, fill us with love:
purify our hearts and lives.

We want to sing your praises, holy God.
But then we let you down by our words.

For those who find it hard to remember
   the feelings and needs of others
     as they give way to destructive anger;
for those who find it hard to know
   what good and helpful and loving things to say
     to those in pain, anxiety or sorrow;
for those who find it hard to express
   their commitment to you and your way
     in words and actions;
we pray:
Spirit of God, fill us with love:
purify our hearts and lives.

In the name of Jesus, who came to reach out
to the sinner, the sick, and the outcast,
and to be the Word of Life to all.   **Amen.**

Faithful God, maker of heaven and earth,
we put our trust in you.

You deal out justice to the oppressed.
We pray for the down-trodden, for . . .
Help us to deal justly with others.
You feed the hungry.
We pray for the starving and malnourished, for . . .
Help us to share with those in need.
In your loving mercy: **Hear our prayer.**

You set the prisoner free.
We pray for those shackled by sin, guilt and fear
and for . . .
Help us to share the gospel of freedom.
You restore sight to the blind.
We pray for those who cannot see the way ahead and for . . .
Help us to share your vision for our lives.
In your loving mercy: **Hear our prayer.**

You raise those who are bowed down.
We pray for the sick, the anxious, the sorrowful, for . . .
Help us to share their heavy load.
You love the righteous.
We pray for all who seek to do your will, for . . .
Help us to live by faith in you.
In your loving mercy: **Hear our prayer.**

You protect the stranger in the land.
We pray for those our society treats as strangers, for . . .
Help us to protect them.
You give support to the fatherless and widow.
We pray for the poor, for . . .
Help us to support them.
In your loving mercy: **Hear our prayer.**

In the name of Jesus, the just and loving.   **Amen.**

God, our wisdom and our truth,
we bring you our words;
   the words of those in authority:
      words that legislate;
            pass judgment;
            persuade;
            make promises.
Word of life, take our words: **and speak through them.**

God, our wisdom and our truth,
we bring you our words;
   the words of those expressing care:
      words that comfort;
            heal;
            bring hope;
            make affirmations of love.
Word of life, take our words: **and speak through them.**

God, our wisdom and our truth,
we bring you our words;
   the words of those who follow Christ:
      words of faith;
            compassion;
            commitment;
            reaching out in reconciliation.
Word of life, take our words: **and speak through them.**

God, our wisdom and our truth,
we bring you our words;
   the words of those who tell others of your gospel:
      words of friendship;
            witness;
            invitation;
            offering salvation.
Word of life, take our words: **and speak through them.**

In the name of Christ, your Word made flesh.   **Amen.**

Loving God, you open the eyes of the blind.
Enlarge our vision.
Save us from self-delusion.
Purify our motives.
Fill us with your Holy Spirit,
that all we say or think or do
may be inspired by you.

Open our eyes to see the damage that we do
as citizens of the world
when, in the name of expediency,
we put our own interests ahead of others.
Silence

Open our eyes to see the damage that we do
within our own families
when, in the name of love,
we seek to possess and mould.
Silence

Open our eyes to see the damage that we do
in caring for other people
when, in the name of concern,
we use them to meet our own needs.
Silence

Open our eyes to see the damage that we do
as members of your church
when, in the name of truth
we fall into bitter disunity.
Silence

Open our eyes, loving God, to see the damage that we do
that we may seek forgiveness
and in the power of your cleansing Spirit,
learn to heal and mend.
May we draw close to you, and you to us.
In the name of Christ, our light and our salvation.   **Amen.**

God of our salvation,
we pray for the members of Christ's body, the church,
asking your help for those who are in any kind of trouble:
  who are anxious
  or have been bereaved;
  whose relationships are in difficulties,
  or who have financial problems;
  for those bowed down by guilt or regret;
  for those being punished for serving you.
We pray for . . .
Loving God: **hear our prayers for one another.**

God of our salvation,
we pray for the members of Christ's body, the church,
asking your healing for those who are ill:
  some unable to be with us;
  some with a long-term illness;
  for those who are in hospital;
  for those facing treatment;
  for those terminally ill;
  for those sick in mind or spirit.
We pray for . . .
Loving God: **hear our prayers for one another.**

God of our salvation,
we pray for the members of Christ's body, the church,
asking for the gift of your Spirit
for those finding the Christian life hard:
  who are questioning their own faith and beliefs or
    are afraid to wholly commit themselves;
  who are distracted by other priorities or
    feel their religion has gone flat;
  for those unable to get along with one another;
  for those in danger of falling away.
We pray for . . .
Loving God: **hear our prayers for one another.**

In Jesus' name.   **Amen.**

Loving God, you have made us for one another.
You sent us your Son, that we might know we are your children.
You sent us your Spirit, to bind us together in love.
God, Three in One and One in Three,
we pray for help with our relationships.

We pray for those whose relationships are going wrong:
    for marriages in trouble;
    for friendships in danger of breaking down;
    for families lacking in love;
    for neighbours in dispute with one another;
    for church members who have fallen out;
    for communities divided by hatred and distrust.
Silence
Creator God: **teach us how to love.**

We pray for the victims of broken relationships:
    for families torn apart;
    for those eaten up by bitterness;
    for children neglected and abused;
    for the lonely and isolated;
    for churches wounded by division;
    for men, women and children injured in civil wars.
Silence
Creator God: **teach us how to love.**

We pray for those making new relationships:
    for the couple falling in love;
    for the strangers becoming friends;
    for those embarking on parenthood;
    for those moving house;
    for those giving their lives to Christ;
    for those building bridges between communities.
Silence
Creator God: **teach us how to love.**

In the name of Jesus our Brother.   **Amen.**

YEAR B – **Sunday between 9/10 & 15/10**

'Good Teacher, what must I do to win eternal life?'

Judge of all, we pray for those whose lives fall short of your standards and who need your help and guidance:
    governments who have failed their people;
    families full of disagreement and misery;
    churches without vision or joy;
    women and men whose lives are empty and meaningless.
Good Teacher, show us what to do to win eternal life.
Help us to seek good and not evil: **that we might live.**

'I have kept all the commandments since I was a boy.'

Ruler of all, we pray for those whose lives are ruled by the observance of duty, and not by love:
    governments who execute justice without mercy;
    families who care for but do not delight in one another;
    churches where doctrine matters more than people;
    women and men who judge and condemn others.
Good Teacher, show us what to do to keep the rule of love.
Help us to seek good and not evil: **that we might live.**

'Go, sell everything you have and give to the poor.
Then come and follow me.'

Saviour of all, we pray for those who long to let go of all that holds them back from following you, yet are afraid:
    governments under the thumb of the wealthy and powerful;
    families burdened by the materialism of society;
    churches unwilling to use their resources to alleviate need;
    women and men who dare not give their lives to you.
Good Teacher, show us what to do to be made new in you.
Help us to seek good and not evil: **that we might live.**

In the name of the Word of God for us, Jesus Christ, our Judge and our Redeemer. **Amen.**

Saving God,
we want the joy and peace and comfort
that come from being disciples of Christ,
but we are reluctant to follow him
along the way of self-offering love.

Saving God,
help us to be willing to drink the cup of suffering with Christ;
to share in the pain of the world he came to save.
We pray
    for the victims of oppression, warfare or violence;
    Silence
    for the lonely, the worried or bereaved;
    Silence
    for the sick in body, mind or spirit;
    Silence
Christ drank the cup of suffering.
Christ bore the pain of the world.
Christ brought healing and peace.
Loving God, make us one with Christ:
make us one with humankind.

Saving God,
help us to be willing to be baptized into death with Christ;
to offer ourselves in the fight against the powers of destruction.
We pray
    for our planet, exploited and polluted;
    Silence
    for communities destroyed by hatred or injustice;
    Silence
    for human beings dying from hunger or neglect;
    Silence
Christ was baptized with the baptism of death.
Christ bore the sin of the world.
Christ brought life and hope.
Loving God, make us one with Christ:
make us one with humankind.   Amen.

Loving God, give us the eyes of faith,
that we may dare to see the world as it is;
that we may dare to see one another's needs;
that we may dare to see with Christ's eyes
   and follow him along his way.
Silence

Son of David, Jesus, have pity on us:
Open our eyes and we will follow you.
We pray that we may not be blind,
or shut our eyes to the suffering of the world:
   to injustice and oppression;
   to hunger and homelessness;
   to violence and torture.
We pray for . . .
Silence

Son of David, Jesus, have pity on us:
Open our eyes and we will follow you.
We pray that we may not be blind,
or shut our eyes to the needs of our neighbours:
   to loneliness and anxiety;
   to illness and depression;
   to bereavement and loss.
We pray for . . .
Silence

Son of David, Jesus, have pity on us:
Open our eyes and we will follow you.
We pray that we may not be blind,
or shut our eyes to visions of you:
   to the majesty of your holiness;
   to the glory of your salvation;
   to the beauty of your love.
Silence

Son of David, Jesus, have pity on us:
Open our eyes and we will follow you.
We pray, in faith, through Christ who heals us.   **Amen.**

God, our father and mother, our creator and saviour,
make us a people of love.
Fill us with love for you.
Fill us with love for one another.
This is our prayer: **help us to know and to do your will.**

Take our hearts, and warm them,
that all our relationships may be transformed
and we may offer acceptance, concern and love
and radiate peace, hope and joy.
This is our prayer: **help us to know and to do your will.**

Take our souls, and nurture them,
that we may grow in goodness and faith
into the full stature of those who live in Christ,
drawing ever closer to you.
This is our prayer: **help us to know and to do your will.**

Take our minds, and enlighten them,
that we may know you as our truth
and share that life-giving knowledge
with words of wisdom and conviction.
This is our prayer: **help us to know and to do your will.**

Take us, and use us,
that the whole of our lives
may be an act of worship
to the glory of your love.
This is our prayer: **help us to know and to do your will.**

God, our hope and our salvation, we pray
that our love for you, and your love for us
may give us the grace to love ourselves
and the courage and understanding to love others.
Teach us to love without counting the cost,
to give our very selves as Christ gave himself for us.
This is our prayer: **help us to know and to do your will.** **Amen.**

Loving God,
we pray for the poor:
    for those who never get enough to eat;
    for those living in shacks or refugee camps;
    for those who cannot afford medicine for their children;
    for those with handicaps that stop them working;
    for . . .
In the name of Jesus Christ, who was rich
but for our sakes became poor: **we pray for the poor.**

Loving God,
we pray for the poor:
    for those destitute and powerless in wealthy lands;
    for those whose poverty has destroyed their self-respect;
    for those who have become despairing, angry, abusive;
    for those who have turned to crime, drugs or drink;
    for . . .
In the name of Jesus Christ, who was rich
but for our sakes became poor: **we pray for the poor.**

Loving God,
we pray for the poor:
    for those whose lives are empty and meaningless;
    for those who are lonely or sad;
    for those who have never felt real joy or peace;
    for those who have never known real love;
    for . . .
In the name of Jesus Christ, who was rich
but for our sakes became poor: **we pray for the poor.**

Loving God,
give us the help and encouragement of your Holy Spirit
that we may learn to give of all that we are and have
so that the world may learn the riches of your love.
In the name of Jesus Christ, who was rich
but for our sakes became poor: **we pray for the poor.**   **Amen.**

Creator God, we pray
for the coming of your kingdom upon earth:
   for the righting of wrongs;
   for the freeing of the oppressed;
   for the ending of wars;
   for the peaceful resolution of conflict;
   for the banishment of poverty and hunger.
Your kingdom come: **your will be done.**

Saviour God, we pray
for a new age for humankind:
   for the righting of distorted values;
   for the freeing of those imprisoned by guilt, fear or despair
   for the ending of hatred and intolerance;
   for peaceful relationships of respect and understanding;
   for the banishment of inhumanity and indifference.
Your kingdom come: **your will be done.**

Spirit of God, we pray
for the renewal of the church:
   for the righting of past betrayals;
   for the freeing of those too afraid to love;
   for the ending of division;
   for the peaceful resolution of disagreements;
   for the banishment of complacency and shallow faith.
Your kingdom come: **your will be done.**

Creator God, we pray for the redemption of creation.
Saviour God, we pray for wholeness for humankind.
Spirit of God, we pray that we may be one with and in you.
Silence

God of past, present and future:
Your kingdom come: **your will be done.**

In the name of Jesus Christ, the new and living way.   **Amen.**

God of power and might,
may your majesty be revealed to the world!
 bring justice!
 bring freedom!
 bring plenty!
 bring joy!
We pray for suffering peoples of the world, for . . .
In your loving mercy: **Hear our prayer.**

God of humility and love,
may your majesty be revealed to humankind!
 bring healing!
 bring peace!
 bring comfort!
 bring new life!
We pray for those who are ill, anxious, or bereaved,
for . . .
In your loving mercy: **Hear our prayer.**

God of life and light,
may your majesty be revealed in our lives!
 bring faith!
 bring wisdom!
 bring courage!
 bring love!
We pray for ourselves, for the church here in . . .
and throughout the world, and especially for . . .
In your loving mercy: **Hear our prayer.**

We pray in the name of Jesus Christ, the faithful witness, the
firstborn from the dead, the ruler of the kings of the earth and our
Lord and Saviour,
In your loving mercy: **Hear our prayer.**   **Amen.**

Year C

Loving God, we pray for those
who are looking forward to better times:
    for nations at war who long for peace;
    for the hungry, desperately awaiting the coming of aid;
    for the oppressed, envisaging a shift in power;
    for the sick, seeking healing and health.
We pray for . . .
Silence
Loving God, hear our prayers.
You are God our Saviour:
In you we put our hope.

Loving God, we pray for those
who believe there is nothing to which they can look forward:
    for those who long only for times past;
    for those who are lonely or depressed;
    for those who feel their lives are stories of failure;
    for those who are chronically or terminally ill.
We pray for . . .
Silence
Loving God, hear our prayers.
You are God our Saviour:
In you we put our hope.

Loving God, we pray for ourselves,
that we may be a forward-looking people:
    ready to respond to each new vision that you give us;
    ready to hear your word for us today;
    ready to be renewed by your Holy Spirit;
    ready to walk boldly into the future with Christ.
We pray for . . .
Silence
Loving God, hear our prayers.
You are God our Saviour:
In you we put our hope.

In the name of Jesus Christ, the Lord our righteousness, who came to
bring the light of hope into our darkness.   **Amen.**

YEAR C – **Second Sunday of Advent**

Creator God,
the children of your world come to you in prayer:
   some hungry –
in your tender compassion: **deliver us;**
   some the victims of war –
in your tender compassion: **deliver us;**
   some poor and oppressed –
in your tender compassion: **deliver us;**
   all of us sinful –
in your tender compassion: **deliver us;**
Creator God, we pray for freedom.

Saviour God,
the children of humanity come to you in prayer:
   some lonely and anxious –
in your tender compassion: **deliver us;**
   some sorrowful or sick –
in your tender compassion: **deliver us;**
   some finding life empty of meaning -
in your tender compassion: **deliver us;**
   all of us sinful –
in your tender compassion: **deliver us;**
Saviour God, we pray for salvation.

Spirit of God,
the children of your church come to you in prayer:
   some suffering in body, mind or spirit –
in your tender compassion: **deliver us;**
   some finding it hard to trust in you –
in your tender compassion: **deliver us;**
   some angry or disillusioned with one another –
in your tender compassion: **deliver us;**
   all of us sinful –
in your tender compassion: **deliver us;**
Spirit of God, we pray for reassurance.

In the name of our mighty saviour, Jesus Christ.   **Amen.**

God our Saviour
we ask for the gift of your Holy Spirit
to help us to prepare for the coming of Christ:
for his birth this Christmas;
for his entry into our hearts;
for his residence in our everyday lives.
May we prove our repentance, our turning towards you,
by the fruit we bear.

*John said, 'Whoever has two shirts must share with him who has
none and whoever has food must do the same.'*

God our Saviour,
we pray for the poor and hungry of our world,
for . . .
May the coming of Christ into our lives
mean clothes for their backs, food for their mouths.

*'And tax collectors said to him, "Teacher, what are we to do?" He
told them, "Exact no more than the assessment."'*

God our Saviour,
we pray for the economically powerless and exploited of our world,
for . . .
May the coming of Christ into our lives
mean fair trade between nations, the lightening of debts.

*'Some soldiers also asked him, "What of us?" To them he said, "No
bullying, no blackmail, make do with your pay."'*

God our Saviour,
we pray for the oppressed and persecuted of our world,
for . . .
May the coming of Christ into our lives
mean liberation, dignity and peace for humankind.

In the name of Jesus Christ, who came to bring new life for the
world. **Amen.**

God Most High,
we pray for the lowly:
   for women living in societies
   where they are regarded as inferior to men –
Mighty God, have mercy:
God our Saviour, show them favour;
   for the powerless, the marginalized
   and those who have no say over their own lives –
Mighty God, have mercy:
God our Saviour, show them favour;
   for children and those dependent upon others
   for care, protection and love –
Mighty God, have mercy:
God our Saviour, show them favour;
   for the gentle, the humble,
   and those who serve you by meeting the needs of others –
Mighty God, have mercy:
God our Saviour, show them favour.

Generous God,
we pray for the hungry:
   for the victims of drought or warfare,
   who have had no harvest –
Mighty God, have mercy:
God our Saviour, show them favour.
   for the destitute, the malnourished,
   who never get enough to eat –
Mighty God, have mercy:
God our Saviour, show them favour.
   for the lonely and loveless,
   deprived of the sustenance of care –
Mighty God, have mercy:
God our Saviour, show them favour.
   for those lacking meaning in their lives
   whose spirits cry out to be fed by you –
Mighty God, have mercy:
God our Saviour, show them favour.
In the name of Jesus Christ.   **Amen.**

'Parenthood brings out the best and worst in me. I never thought I would feel so loving and protective . . . or get so angry! The intensity . . . and the responsibility . . . of parenthood can feel quite overwhelming.'

God, our mother and our father,
we pray for the parents of young children:
for new mothers and fathers, coming to terms with unimagined joys
    and demands;
for those confused by conflicting views on the upbringing of
    children;
for those whose children have physical, mental or emotional
    disabilities;
for those whose own loveless or abusive childhoods have left them
    unable to truly love.
God, our mother and our father,
we pray for the parents of young children;
In your love and mercy: **hear our prayer.**

'I love my parents and I know and am grateful that they love me. But they don't have to feel so responsible for me any more. I need to feel free to find and be myself!'

God, our mother and our father,
we pray for growing children:
for those coming to terms with the unimagined joys and demands
    of growing up;
for those confused by discovering other values than those of their
    parents;
for those longing for independence but held back by physical,
    mental or emotional disabilities;
for those whose inner growth has been stunted by lack of love or
    by abuse.
God, our mother and our father,
we pray for growing children;
In your love and mercy: **hear our prayer.**
We have welcomed the Christchild into our world and into our lives
this Christmas. We pray that his love may grow to maturity within
us, so that we, like him, may reach our full stature as your children.
In our Brother's name.   **Amen.**.

Loving God,
we pray for your church:
    for all those baptized into the household of faith.
Come, Holy Spirit, come to your people;
comfort us, encourage us: **fire us with your love.**

We pray for the worldwide church:
    for the poor, the hungry, those caught up in conflict;
    for the powerless, persecuted, exploited or oppressed;
    for . . .
Come, Holy Spirit, come to your people;
comfort us, encourage us: **fire us with your love.**

We pray for the church in this society:
    for the unity that witnesses to the love of Christ;
    for a deeper concern to meet human needs;
    for . . .
Come, Holy Spirit, come to your people;
comfort us, encourage us: **fire us with your love.**

We pray for this congregation:
    for a wise and loving nurture of the young in faith;
    for those who are ill, sorrowful or anxious;
    for . . .
Come, Holy Spirit, come to your people;
comfort us, encourage us: **fire us with your love**

We pray for ourselves:
    that we may remain faithful to the baptismal promises;
    that we may hold fast to your promises to us.
Come, Holy Spirit, come to your people;
comfort us, encourage us: **fire us with your love.**

In the name of your beloved Son, Jesus Christ, our Brother and our
Saviour. **Amen.**

Loving God, we bring to you in prayer
those whose resources are running out:
   the poor and the hungry
   Silence
   those tiring in the struggle for justice
   Silence
   countries burdened with heavy debts.
   Silence
Show us what we should do to help.
Call us, change us, use us.
Your kingdom come: **your will be done.**

Loving God, we bring to you in prayer
those who feel their resources for living running low:
   the ill and the infirm
   Silence
   the sorrowful and despairing
   Silence
   the stressed and exhausted.
   Silence
Show us what we should do to help.
Call us, change us, use us.
Your kingdom come: **your will be done.**

Loving God, we come to you in prayer
to ask for the resources we need for Christian living:
   for faith and courage
   Silence
   for wisdom and love
   Silence
   for the gifts of your Holy Spirit
     which will equip us to fulfill
     our individual callings from you.
   Silence
Call us, change us, use us.
Your kingdom come: **your will be done,**
in Christ's name, and to your glory.   **Amen.**

God of the living, of the present moment,
your word contains truth for each new generation.
We pray for fresh and exciting reminders
of the power and glory of your sovereign love.

Speak to us anew, living God,
of your concern for justice for the poor and oppressed.
Help us to announce your good news;
      to proclaim your liberty to those held captive;
      to work and pray for a better world.

This is our prayer: **Amen, Amen.**

Speak to us anew, living God,
of the ways in which you want us to live.
Help us to share the hope we have in you;
      to proclaim your love for every individual;
      to work and pray for new life for humankind.

This is our prayer: **Amen, Amen.**

Speak to us anew, living God,
of our calling as members of Christ's body.
Help us to be united in love and respect for one another;
      to proclaim your salvation to the world;
      to work and pray under the guidance of your Spirit.

This is our prayer: **Amen, Amen.**

We make our prayers in the name of your Son,
Jesus Christ, the Word made flesh,
who brought new life to old words
and to old ways of living,
who announced the good news of our salvation.   **Amen.**

'Love is patient and kind.'
We pray for the victims of impatience or unkindness:
    those who take longer to do or understand things,
      or who find it hard to adapt to new ways;
    those smarting from an injustice,
      or wounded by cruel words.   *Silence*
Gracious God: **fill us with your love.**

'Love envies no one, is never boastful, never conceited, never rude.'
We pray for the victims of envy or pride:
    those who are never satisfied with what they have,
      or who are too satisfied with who they are;
    those trodden underfoot in the clamber for success,
      belittled by lack of respect from others.   *Silence*
Gracious God: **fill us with your love.**

'Love is never selfish, never quick to take offence.'
We pray for the victims of selfishness or anger:
    those who live in poverty and hunger,
      or whose deepest needs are never met;
    those left lonely and bereft after a quarrel,
      longing for reconciliation and peace.   *Silence*
Gracious God: **fill us with your love.**

'Love keeps no score of wrongs, takes no pleasure in the sins of others, but delights in the truth.'
We pray for the victims of sin or falsehood:
    those whose unloving deeds have ruined their own lives
      and the lives of those around them;
    those whose lives have been built upon and shaped
      by wrong ideas of truth and false priorities.   *Silence.*
Gracious God: **fill us with your love.**

'There is nothing love cannot face; there is no limit to its faith, its hope, its endurance.'
Gracious God: **fill us with your love.   Amen.**

'The people of God are called to be prophets. . .'
God of power and holiness,
we pray for those whom you have entrusted
with prophetic messages for your world:
   the man called to speak out against
   a government that is cruel, oppressive and unjust;
   the woman called to go into politics
   to speak out for those whose voice is weak;
   the young person called to speak out to the church
   to challenge, to question, to provoke thought.
Loving God, open the ears of your people:
that we may truly hear.

'The people of God are called to be disciples. . .'
God of wisdom and salvation,
we pray for the church which you have entrusted
with the truths and tenets of the faith:
   the woman starting out on her Christian journey
   eager to learn of you and your way of love;
   the man whose faith is being tested
   by illness, bereavement, the suffering of others;
   the young person who longs to follow you
   but whose beliefs are ridiculed by friends.
Loving God, open the ears of your people:
that we may truly hear.

'The people of God are called to be apostles. . .'
God of inspiration and love,
we pray for your children whom you have entrusted
with the gospel of your unfailing love:
   the man called to witness to your love
   by offering caring concern to those around him;
   the woman called to preach the good news
   and rouse the faithful to share it with others;
   the young person expressing faith
   through responding to the cries of those in need.
Loving God, open the ears of your people:
that we may truly hear.   Amen.

Unchanging God,
help us to put our trust in you.

We pray for those
who have put their trust in governments
and been let down:
for the destitute, the exploited, the victims of injustice;
for . . .
In your love and mercy: **Hear our prayer.**

We pray for those
who have put their trust in material success
and been let down:
for those who, in gaining wealth, have lost true riches;
for . . .
In your love and mercy: **Hear our prayer.**

We pray for those
who have put their trust in those they love
and been let down:
for the betrayed, the neglected, the victims of abuse;
for . . .
In your love and mercy: **Hear our prayer.**

We pray for those
who have put their trust in their own strength
and been let down:
for those unable to cope with suffering, failure or loss;
for . . .
In your love and mercy: **Hear our prayer.**

We pray that we may be truly blessed
as we put our trust in you
and build our lives
upon the sure and steady foundation of your love.
In your love and mercy: **Hear our prayer.**
We pray in faith, in the assurance that Jesus Christ is our crucified
and risen Saviour.   **Amen.**

Creator God, we ask that you might reveal to your world
the true meaning and power of love:
　　love that seeks justice
　　　　and is merciful and compassionate;
　　love that destroys enmity
　　　　and promotes harmony and peace;
　　love that banishes hunger
　　　　and shares with those in need.
We pray for the people of . . .
Gracious God, we delight in you:
Grant us our hearts' desire.

Saviour God, we ask that you might reveal to humankind
the true meaning and power of love:
　　love that does not judge
　　　　but pardons and restores;
　　love that is not limited
　　　　but all-consuming and overflowing;
　　love that cannot be destroyed
　　　　but brings healing and new life.
We pray for those burdened by guilt or fear,
by loneliness, sorrow, or illness, for . . .
Gracious God, we delight in you:
Grant us our hearts' desire.

Spirit of God, we ask that you might reveal to your church
the true meaning and power of love:
　　love that unites
　　　　and overcomes disagreement and hurt;
　　love that builds up
　　　　and offers acceptance and encouragement;
　　love that witnesses to itself
　　　　and speaks out about the gospel.
We pray for the church throughout the world,
and for this congregation in . . . for . . .
Gracious God, we delight in you:
Grant us our hearts' desire.
In Jesus' name.　**Amen.**

YEAR C – Sunday between 25/2 & 29/2 or 24/5 & 28/5

God of justice,
   when we pray to you for justice
      for the oppressed and exploited of our world;
   when we pray to you for succour
      for the hungry and the homeless,
hear our prayers;
and help us to listen to what we are asking,
that our prayers might change us, too.
Lord, Lord, speak to us:
and help us to act on your words.

God of salvation,
   when we pray to you for forgiveness
      for those burdened by guilt and sin;
   when we pray to you for healing and comfort
      for those who are suffering or sorrowful,
hear our prayers;
and help us to listen to what we are asking,
that our prayers might change us, too.
Lord, Lord, speak to us:
and help us to act on your words.

God of love,
   when we pray to you for unity
      for the church and for congregations scarred by disagreement;
   when we pray to you for one another
      for those needing your strength and guidance,
hear our prayers;
and help us to listen to what we are asking,
that our prayers might change us, too.
Lord, Lord, speak to us:
and help us to act on your words.

In the name of Jesus Christ, our Teacher and Saviour, who makes us
one with God, with one another, and with ourselves.   **Amen.**

Holy God,
when we are dazzled by your holiness,
    taken aback by your glory,
    overwhelmed by your presence
    and unsure how to respond,
draw the veil from our eyes, that we may perceive
what you, in your holiness, want of us.
Your holiness demands justice:
help us to work and pray for those unfairly treated.
Your holiness demands mercy:
help us to work and pray for those who have done wrong.
Your holiness demands compassion:
help us to work and pray for those in need.
Your holiness demands right living:
help us to work and pray for respect and consideration
   between individuals, communities and nations.
In your love and mercy: **hear our prayer.**

Loving God,
when we are dazzled by your love,
    taken aback by your vulnerability,
    overwhelmed by your presence
    and unsure how to respond,
draw the veil from our eyes, that we may perceive
what you, in your love, are offering to humankind.
Your love offers forgiveness:
help us to work and pray for reconciliation.
Your love offers healing:
help us to work and pray for those who are ill or in pain.
Your love offers hope:
help us to work and pray for those who are sorrowful.
Your love offers new life to all:
Help us to work and pray for your love's sake,
   that the world may see and believe.
In your love and mercy: **hear our prayer.**
In the name of your Son, our glorious Saviour,
Jesus Christ. **Amen.**

'The devil said to Jesus "If you are the Son of God, command this stone to become a loaf of bread." Jesus answered him, "It is written 'One does not live by bread alone.'"'
Creator God,
we pray that the hungry may be fed
and that they may know the deeper satisfaction
that comes from being enabled to feed themselves.
We pray that the ill may be made well
and that they may know the deeper wholeness
that comes from your healing touch on human lives.
Silence

'The devil said "If you will worship me all the kingdoms of the world will be yours." Jesus answered "It is written 'Worship the Lord your God and serve him alone.'"'
Saviour God,
we pray for the leaders of our world,
that they may not exercise power for its own sake,
but with wisdom, justice and compassion.
We pray for those who feel powerless
in the face of death, suffering and sin
that they may know the power of your saving love.
Silence

'The devil said "If you are the Son of God, throw yourself from this pinnacle." Jesus answered "It is said 'Do not put the Lord your God to the test.'"'
Spirit of God,
we pray that our faith
may not only give us comfort and security
but challenge us to follow Christ's way of suffering love.
We pray that our faith
might stand the tests of time and trouble
and offer hope to those around us.
Silence
We make our prayers in the name of Jesus Christ, who was tempted,
as we are, but remained faithful to the end.   **Amen.**

YEAR C – **Second Sunday in Lent**

God, our light and our salvation, we pray for your help,
when life is a struggle and the way ahead is hard.

We pray for:
    those campaigning for justice for a people
        suffering under an uncaring regime;
    those working amongst homeless refugees
        providing food, medical treatment, support;
    the peoples of . . .
Hear our prayer, loving God: **we put our hope in you.**

We pray for:
    those weakened by illness,
        afraid of what the future may hold;
    those who have lost a loved companion,
        whose lives are overshadowed by grief;
    for . . .
Hear our prayer, loving God: **we put our hope in you.**

We pray for:
    those haunted by doubt and despair,
        facing the future with little faith;
    those seeking the new life to be found in you,
        but holding back from total commitment;
    for . . .
Hear our prayer, loving God: **we put our hope in you.**

We pray in silence for
    ourselves, and bring to you
    our fears, our anxieties, our pain.
Silence
God, our light and our salvation, we pray for your help,
when life is a struggle, the way ahead hard.
Hear our prayer, loving God: **we put our hope in you.**

In the name of Jesus Christ, who set his face towards Jerusalem,
suffering and death that we might know joy and salvation.　**Amen.**

Creator God,
you call the rulers of the nations to repentance.
You call them to leave behind their old ways
of injustice, oppression, greed and conflict
and turn to you;
to seek justice, freedom, plenty and peace
for the peoples with whom they are entrusted.
Creator God, we pray
that the rulers of the nations might turn to you.
Let the wicked abandon their ways:
and the evil their thoughts.

Saviour God,
you call humankind to repentance.
You call us to leave behind our old ways of living,
our selfishness, guilt, anxiety and despair
and turn to you;
to seek love, forgiveness, comfort and hope,
to find a new and everlasting life.
Saviour God, we pray
that humankind might turn to you.
Let the wicked abandon their ways:
and the evil their thoughts.

Spirit of God,
you call the church to repentance.
You call us to leave behind our old failings,
our disagreements, intolerance, apathy and fear
and turn to you;
to seek unity, love, vision and courage
that the world might see and believe.
Spirit of God, we pray
that the church might turn to you.
Let the wicked abandon their ways:
and the evil their thoughts.

In the name of your Son, Jesus Christ,
who came to seek and to save the lost.   **Amen.**

Loving Father God, we pray
for those who have left behind
the people whom they love:
for those who have left home
to start a new job or a new course of learning,
or to set up a new home;
for those forced to leave
by the breakdown of a relationship;
for those who have left with nowhere to go,
who feel lonely, lost or afraid.
Silence
And we pray, too, for those left behind:
the parents who have said goodbye to their children;
the children who have said goodbye to a parent;
the partners who are separating;
the bereaved left desolate and alone.
Silence

Loving Mother God, we pray
for those who have turned their back
on you and on your love:
those who feel they can no longer believe in you
because of the evil and suffering in the world;
those too caught up in the business of living
to think about the true meaning of life;
those who feel they can no longer come to you
because they are tainted with guilt, anger or despair.
Silence
And we pray, too, for the church:
that we might show your love to the world;
that we might challenge the standards of the world;
that we might offer your forgiveness to the world
and share the good news of your victory over sin and death.
Silence

In the name of your Son, Jesus Christ,
who died and rose again that we might know ourselves
your forgiven, beloved daughters and sons.   **Amen.**

Compassionate Parent God,
your children are weeping:
   they weep because they are hungry and poor;
   they weep because they are caught up in war;
   they weep because they are powerless and exploited.
We pray for . . .
We share their sorrows.
May we help them, comfort them, offer them hope.
Saving God, we pray that those who sow in tears:
may reap with songs of joy.

Compassionate Saviour God,
our sisters and brothers are weeping:
   they weep because they are ill or in pain;
   they weep because someone they love has died;
   they weep from guilt, emptiness or anger.
We pray for . . .
We share their sorrows.
May we help them, comfort them, offer them hope.
Saving God, we pray that those who sow in tears:
may reap with songs of joy.

Compassionate, sustaining God,
your people are weeping:
   they weep because they have let you down;
   they weep because they have let others down;
   they weep because loving hurts.
We pray for . . .
Their sorrows are ours.
Help us, comfort us, fill us with faith and hope.
Saving God, we pray that those who sow in tears:
may reap with songs of joy.

In the name of Jesus Christ, our Joy and our Salvation.   **Amen.**

**Sixth Sunday in Lent
(Palm Sunday)**

Jesus – riding into Jerusalem on a donkey.
Loving God, we pray for the leaders of the nations and their
peoples, for . . .
Your kingdom come: **your will be done.**

Jesus – sharing a last meal with his friends.
Loving God, we pray that we may be faithful and humble friends to
one another.
Your kingdom come: **your will be done.**

Jesus – praying on the Mount of Olives.
Loving God, we pray for those seeking your strength and guidance
at times of anxiety and fear, for . . .
Your kingdom come: **your will be done.**

Jesus – being betrayed by Judas, denied by Peter.
Loving God, we pray that we may remain faithful to you through
all the testing times in our lives.
Your kingdom come: your will be done.

Jesus – being tried by the authorities.
Loving God, we pray for those who face condemnation for doing
what they believe you want them to do, for . . .
Your kingdom come: **your will be done.**

Jesus – being condemned to death by the crowd.
Loving God, we pray for the courage to stand up for our faith in
you.
Your kingdom come: **your will be done.**

Jesus – being crucified and suffering.
Loving God, we pray for those we know, who are suffering
physically, emotionally, mentally, for . . .
Your kingdom come: **your will be done.**

Jesus – dying upon the cross.
Loving God, may we love you to the end of our lives.
Your kingdom come: **your will be done.   Amen.**

'When there is nothing left to look forward to, there are still things to be done. We will go to the tomb and anoint his body. But our hope is dead.'
Let us pray for those who live in despair,
who go through the motions of living
with no joy in their hearts:
the poor and hungry, in their daily dehumanizing struggle;
the lonely and loveless, who have no sense of self worth;
the empty and depressed, for whom life is meaningless.
Jesus Christ is the Lord of hope:
  he has burst out of the tomb of despair.
God of life and hope: **Raise us with Christ.**

'When goodness has been defeated by evil, love by hatred and life has died, we will go and mourn at the tomb. But where can we place our faith now?'
Let us pray for those who feel defeated,
whose plans and dreams for the future
have been erased and shattered:
the workers for justice driven underground;
the seriously ill whose recovery is doubtful or slow;
the partners in a relationship that is breaking down.
Jesus Christ is the Lord of love:
  he has burst out of the tomb of defeat.
God of life and hope: **Raise us with Christ.**

'When the one we love has died and our hearts are full of pain and grief, we will go to the tomb and shed our tears. But where shall we go for comfort?'
God of life and hope, we pray for those who are bereaved,
their lives shattered by a loss
that leaves them shocked, confused, angry and in pain:
for those who grieve for someone they love;
for those uprooted from home, family and friends;
for those whose faith in you has died.
Jesus Christ is the Lord of life:
  he has burst out of the tomb of death.
God of life and hope: **Raise us with Christ.**   **Amen.**

YEAR C – Second Sunday of Easter

Creator God,
we pray for the world
on days in which it is hard to believe that
   the hungry will be fed,
   there will be justice and freedom,
   and that wars will cease.

We pray for the world
on days when we cannot see you within it.
We pray for faith: **may your peace be with us.**

Saviour God,
we pray for humankind
on days in which it is hard to believe that
   love is stronger than hatred,
   the sick will be made well,
   and that death has been destroyed.

We pray for humankind
on days when we cannot see you among us.
We pray for faith: **may your peace be with us.**

Spirit of God,
we pray for the church
on days in which it is hard to believe that
   we have a message for the world,
   our unity is greater than our division,
   and that we will ever serve you as we should.

We pray for the church
on days when we cannot see you at work within it.
We pray for faith: **may your peace be with us.**

Jesus said 'Be unbelieving no longer, but believe.'
We pray to you because we have faith
in the love made known to us
in the life, death and resurrection of your Son,
our Saviour, Jesus Christ.   **Amen.**

'Jesus said to Simon Peter, "Simon, son of John, do you love me . . .?" "Yes, Lord," he answered, "you know that I love you." "Then feed my lambs," he said.'

Lord, you know that we love you
and we know that we can show you that love
by loving one another and all the world.

We pray for the world,
where people hunger after justice,
          long for freedom,
          crave for peace;
where people are hungry,
          homeless,
          destitute.
Lord, help us to feed your lambs.
In your love and mercy: **hear our prayer.**

We pray for humankind,
for those who are ill in body or mind,
          anxious and afraid,
          depressed and despairing;
for those who are grieving,
          lonely,
          abused.
Lord, help us to tend your sheep.
In your love and mercy: **hear our prayer.**

We pray for ourselves, your followers and friends,
asking that we may be filled with your Holy Spirit
and given those things that we need
to feed the physical, spiritual and emotional hungers
of the world around us.
Lord, help us to feed your sheep.
In your love and mercy: **hear our prayer.**

In the name of Jesus Christ, the Good Shepherd,
who lay down his life for his sheep.   **Amen.**

Loving Shepherd of your sheep,
we pray for those who hunger for love:
   may they lie down in the green pastures of your care.
Silence
We pray for those who thirst for peace:
   may they drink of you and find rest.
Silence
We pray for those whose spirits are weary:
   may they be revived by you.
Silence

Loving Shepherd of your sheep,
we remember before you those walking
through valleys of deepest darkness:
   those who are ill;
   those who have been bereaved;
   those overshadowed by guilt or depression;
   those who are lonely or afraid.
We pray for . . .
asking that they might know that you are with them
   and fear no harm;
asking that they might know the comfort
   of your guiding, protecting and saving love.

Loving Shepherd of your sheep,
you have provided us with all that we need.
You have blessed us richly.
We ask for the grace and wisdom
   to respond to your love and goodness
   by putting our faith in you.
We ask for the grace and courage
   to follow you along the path of self-giving love
   all the days of our lives.

In the name of him who keeps us safe,
Jesus Christ our Lord and Saviour.   **Amen.**

God of justice and compassion,
we pray for the rulers of the world,
    that they may not put the practice of economic theories
    or the fulfilment of political ideologies
    before their duty to meet the needs of their people.
Guided by your Holy Spirit, may they seek
    peace, and not warfare,
    justice, and not the wielding of power for its own sake,
    to feed the hungry rather hoarding wealth.
We pray for . . .
Open our lives to your Spirit:
open our hearts to love one another.

God of generosity and forgiveness,
we pray for human beings and their relationships,
    that we may not put our own rights,
    our own wants and desires
    before the rights and needs of those around us.
Guided by your Holy Spirit, may we be
    loving and giving,
    tolerant and respectful,
    forgiving and accepting.
We pray for . . .
Open our lives to your Spirit:
open our hearts to love one another.

God of love and life,
we pray for the church,
    that we may not put our own dogmas
    our traditions and prejudices
    before our love for one another and the world.
Guided by your Holy Spirit, may we be
    united in our witness to the gospel,
    welcoming to all,
    open to new visions of what we should do.
We pray for . . .
Open our lives to your Spirit:
open our hearts to love one another.   Amen.

YEAR C – **Sixth Sunday of Easter**

Let us pray for the mission of the church,
for the fulfillment of her calling
to spread the good news of Jesus Christ.

Saving God,
we pray for those, like Paul,
who witness to the gospel
by word and deed
amongst strangers:
   for evangelists and missionaries,
   for . . .
   for aid workers in desperate situations,
   for . . .
   for ourselves, in our conversations and dealings
   with people we have just met.
Spirit of God, give us wisdom, courage and love
that we may be true apostles of Christ.
Let the peoples praise you, God:
let all peoples praise you.

Saving God,
we pray for those, like Lydia,
who witness to the gospel
by word and deed
amongst those with whom they live and work:
   for ministers and lay workers
   for . . .
   for those in the caring professions
   for . . .
   for ourselves, in our conversations and relationships
   with those we know and love.
Spirit of God, give us wisdom, courage and love
that we may be true disciples of Christ.
Let the peoples praise you, God:
let all peoples praise you.

In the name of Jesus Christ,
the light of our lives and the Light of the World.   **Amen.**

Loving God, make us one,
   that the world may know Jesus Christ.

Loving God, make us one
   with the African Christian praying for peace;
   with the Chinese Christian praying for freedom;
   with the South American Christian praying for justice;
   with the Asian Christian praying for food;
   with . . .
Unite us in faith: **unite us in love.**

Loving God, make us one
   with the sick man praying for healing;
   with the guilt-ridden woman praying for forgiveness;
   with the bewildered teenager praying for guidance;
   with the bereaved child, praying for comfort;
   with . . .
Unite us in faith: **unite us in love.**

Loving God, make us one
   in our prayers for church unity;
   in our concern for the world;
   in our service to the community;
   in our witness to your love;
   in . . .
Unite us in faith: **unite us in love.**

Loving God, make us one
   to love and care for one another;
   to treat each other with tolerance and respect;
   to learn from one another and grow together;
   that we may truly worship and serve you;
   that . . .
Unite us in faith: **unite us in love.**

We pray in the name of him to whom we have been entrusted,
in the name of Jesus Christ, your Son,
our Brother and our Saviour.   **Amen.**

Creator God, we pray for the world,
where words are used
    to order the destruction of people and property;
    to seduce and deceive electorates;
    to cover up corruption and wrongdoing;
    to incite hatred and create division.
Creator God, we long to hear words of peace,
                  of truth,
                  of justice
                  of love.
Holy Spirit, Spirit of truth and love:
Speak to us and speak through us.

Saviour God, we pray for those who suffer,
when words are used
    to give news of illness;
    to say goodbye to loved ones;
    to lash out in anger and frustration;
    to pass moral judgments on others.
Saviour God, we long to hear words of healing,
                  of comfort
                  of forgiveness
                  of love.
Holy Spirit, Spirit of truth and love:
Speak to us and speak through us.

God in us, we pray for the church,
that words may be used
    to bind us together in love for you and one another;
    to witness to the good news of Jesus Christ;
    to speak out against injustice and inhumanity;
    to share our visions and dreams of your kingdom.
God in us, we long to hear your words of power,
                  of hope,
                  of joy,
                  of love.
Holy Spirit, Spirit of truth and love:
Speak to us and speak through us.   Amen.

'We are at peace with God through our Lord Jesus Christ.'

Loving God, our parent, our saviour, Spirit of peace,
we thank you for the gift of peace;
that through our Lord Jesus Christ
we can be at peace with you, with one another,
with ourselves.
We pray for those who are not at peace:
for those who live in a turmoil
of guilt towards and anger with you;
  for those who live in conflict
  with family, friends or neighbours;
  for those wracked by anxiety,
    ill at ease with themselves.
Silence
Loving God, our parent, our saviour, Spirit of peace,
give them your peace that passes understanding.

'Through the Holy Spirit he has given us, God's love has flooded our hearts.'

Loving God, our parent, our saviour, Spirit of love,
we thank you for the gift of love,
with which, through the Holy Spirit,
you have renewed and transformed our lives.
We pray for those who long for love:
  for those who seek you,
  and your parental, saving and empowering love;
  for those who are lonely,
  neglected or abused;
  for those with little self respect,
  hesitant in embracing the challenge of loving.
Silence
Loving God, our parent, our saviour, Spirit of love,
give them the knowledge of your love that never dies.   **Amen.**

Word of God,
speak of holiness to your world:
   speak of justice;
   speak of righteousness;
   speak of freedom;
   speak of compassion.
God of power and love, say the word:
and we will be made whole.

Word of God,
speak of hope to those who suffer:
   speak of healing;
   speak of comfort;
   speak of strength;
   speak of eternal life.
God of power and love, say the word:
and we will be made whole.

Word of God,
speak of truth to humankind:
   speak of forgiveness;
   speak of faith;
   speak of openness;
   speak of life's meaning.
God of power and love, say the word:
and we shall be made whole.

Word of God,
speak of love to your people:
   speak of acceptance;
   speak of renewal;
   speak of sacrifice;
   speak of joy.
God of power and love, say the word:
and we shall be made whole.

In the name of Jesus Christ,
your Word made flesh.   **Amen.**

You, loving God, have the power
to turn our lives around!
You provided food for your prophet Elijah
and the widow of Zarephath
when they were about to die of hunger.
We pray for those desperate
for their lives to be turned around:
    the hungry, poor or homeless;
    those caught up in wars and conflicts;
    those living under unjust regimes.
We pray especially for . . .

You, loving God, have the power
to turn our lives around!
Through Christ you raised
the son of the widow of Nain
back to life.
We pray for those aching
for their lives to be turned around:
    the anxious, fearful and despairing;
    those ill in body, mind or spirit;
    those whose lives are darkened by loss.
We pray especially for . . .

You, loving God, have the power
to turn our lives around!
You revealed Jesus as your Son
to Paul on the road to Damascus,
and turned him from persecutor into apostle.
We pray for those searching for the truth
that will turn their lives around:
    the guilt-ridden or those with empty lives;
    those just embarking on a relationship with you;
    those struggling with apathy or doubt.
We pray especially for . . .

In the name of him who came to bring us newness of life,
your Son, our Saviour, Jesus Christ.   **Amen.**

Creator God,
   help us to seek justice
   not only for ourselves, but for others.
Make us aware not only of our rights
but also of the needs of other people.
We remember before you:
   the poor;
   the homeless;
   the down-trodden;
and pray for justice for all humankind.
In your love and mercy: **hear our prayer.**

Saviour God,
   help us to seek forgiveness
   not only for ourselves, but to offer to others.
Make us aware that we not only need to be right with you
but that we also need to be right with one another.
We remember before you:
   those who feel guilty;
   those whom we have wronged;
   those in relationships that are in trouble;
and pray that we and they might know forgiveness.
In your love and mercy: **hear our prayer.**

Spirit of God,
   help us to seek love
   not only for ourselves, but to give to others.
Make us aware not only of our own feelings
but also of the feelings of other people.
We remember before you:
   the lonely;
   the suffering;
   the sorrowful;
and pray that the healing and comforting power of your love might
be shown and known.
In your love and mercy: **hear our prayer.**
In the name of Jesus Christ, who came that we might know your
forgiving love for all humankind.   **Amen.**

'There is no such thing as Jew and Greek;
. . . for you are all one person in Christ Jesus.'

Loving God, Three in One and One in Three,
we pray for the breaking down of barriers between Christians:
barriers of race;
       of culture;
       of tradition.
Silence
We belong to Christ:
make us one in him.

'There is no such thing as . . . slave and freeman;
. . . for you are all one person in Christ Jesus.'

Loving God, Three in One and One in Three,
we pray for the breaking down of barriers between Christians:
barriers of class;
       of income;
       of power.
Silence
We belong to Christ:
make us one in him.

'There is no such thing as . . . male and female;
. . . for you are all one person in Christ Jesus.'

Loving God, Three in One and One in Three,
we pray for the breaking down of barriers between Christians:
barriers of gender;
       of age;
       of physical and mental ability.
Silence
We belong to Christ:
make us one in him.

Loving God, in Christ's name we pray – break down the barriers of
fear, distrust and pride.   **Amen.**

Creator God,
we pray for the world,
asking that those with power, wealth or influence
might show commitment
to the welfare of their peoples and communities;
might show commitment
to your principles of:
    justice and freedom;
    mercy and compassion;
    peace and understanding.
We pray for . . .
In your love and mercy: **hear our prayer.**

Saviour God,
we pray for humankind,
asking that each of us, young or old, rich or poor,
might show commitment
to caring for one another;
might show commitment
to your desire that we should
    care for those who are ill;
    comfort those who are sad;
    feed those who are hungry;
    befriend those who are alone.
We pray for . . .
In your love and mercy: **hear our prayer.**

Spirit of God,
we pray for the church,
asking that the family of Christ
might show commitment
to you and to your way;
might show the commitment that leads to:
    love, joy, peace and patience;
    kindness, goodness and fidelity;
    gentleness and self-control.
We pray for . . .
In your love and mercy: **hear our prayer.**   **Amen.**

Loving God, teach us how to be apostles of Christ.
We pray for those living out their Christian calling
in the political arena:
for those involved in local government,
for . . .
for those involved in national government,
for . . .
for Christian leaders and politicians
in countries overseas, for . . .
Your kingdom come: **your will be done.**

Loving God, teach us how to be apostles of Christ.
We pray for those living out their Christian calling
in the service of those in need:
for aid workers helping victims of famine or warfare,
for . . .
for medical staff, seeking to heal and to alleviate pain,
for . . .
for ourselves, as we seek to comfort and encourage
the sorrowful, the anxious and the lonely,
for . . .
Your kingdom come: **your will be done.**

Loving God, teach us how to be apostles of Christ.
We pray for those living out their Christian calling
by sharing the good news of Jesus:
for evangelists, preachers and teachers,
for . . .
for broadcasters, musicians and writers,
for . . .
for ourselves, that by our words and our deeds
we may invite others to put on the easy yoke of Christ,
for . . .
Your kingdom come: **your will be done.**

In the name of him through whom we have been made a new
creation, Jesus Christ, our Lord and Saviour. **Amen.**

God, our fellow traveller,
we pray for those setting out on a journey,
   holiday makers . . .
   families moving home . . .
   refugees . . .
and for those setting out on a new journey of life,
   babies and children . . .
   young people leaving home . . .
   new Christians . . .
Encircle them with love.
Protect and guide them.
In your love and mercy: **hear our prayer.**

God, our fellow traveller,
we pray for those injured on a journey,
   the victims of crime . . .
   the victims of accidents . . .
   the victims of disease . . .
and for those wounded on the journey of life,
   children neglected and abused . . .
   those ill in body, mind or spirit . . .
   the bereaved, the anxious or despairing . . .
Bind up their wounds.
Comfort and strengthen them.
In your love and mercy: **hear our prayer.**

God, our fellow traveller,
we pray for those who help us on our journeys,
   workers in the tourist industry . . .
   strangers who befriend us and lend a hand . . .
   aid workers amongst the homeless and destitute . . .
and for those who help us along the journey of life
   our family and friends
   teachers, preachers, counsellors,
   the household of faith.
Keep us travelling together.
Unite us in your love.
In your love and mercy: **hear our prayer.   Amen.**

Creator God,
your world is a busy place;
its leaders fret and fuss about so many things.
Creator God,
teach them the things that are necessary:
   justice for the oppressed and exploited;
   compassion for the hungry and destitute;
   peace between individuals, communities and nations.
We pray that they may choose what is best.
God of our lives: **help us to put your kingdom first.**

Saviour God,
people are often very busy,
they fret and fuss about so many things.
Saviour God,
teach them the things that are necessary:
   healthy and loving relationships;
   purpose and spiritual depth in life;
   caring for those who need comfort and help.
We pray that they may choose what is best.
God of our lives: **help us to put your kingdom first.**

Spirit of God,
your church is a busy community,
fretting and fussing about so many things.
Spirit of God,
teach your church the things that are necessary:
   a joyful and obedient faith in you;
   unity in love for one another;
   self-giving love for your world.
We pray that your church may choose what is best.
God of our lives: **help us to put your kingdom first.**

In the name of Jesus Christ, your image and your dear Son,
our Teacher and our Saviour.   **Amen.**

'Father, may your name be hallowed; your kingdom come.'
We know you, Father, as 'God of Justice',
 and so we pray for those who are unjustly treated, for . . .
we know you as 'God of Mercy',
 and so we pray for compassion for the needy, for . . .
we know you as 'God of Love',
 and so we pray for peace where there is conflict, for . . .
You are our God: we are your people.
May we hallow your name with our lips and our lives.
Your kingdom come: **your will be done.**

'Give us each day our daily bread.'
We pray for those who do not have enough to eat today . . .
asking that they may be fed.
We pray for those hungry for love and friendship,
 for forgiveness, peace, or a sense of purpose;
asking that they may be fed.
We pray that we might be given the daily spiritual food
that we need in order to meet the needs of other people.
Your kingdom come: **your will be done.**

'And forgive us our sins,
 for we too forgive all who have done us wrong.'
We pray for those who have hurt us . . .
asking that we might absorb that hurt and not return it.
We pray for relationships where there is discord.
We pray for the church, that we may be made one.
Your kingdom come: **your will be done.**

'And do not put us to the test.'
We pray for those going through trying times:
 those who are ill, or anxious, for . . .
 those who have been bereaved, for . . .
 those facing big challenges, for . . .
asking that they, and we, may receive from you
strength and guidance, comfort and hope.
Your kingdom come: **your will be done.**
We make our prayers in obedience to Jesus Christ.   **Amen.**

Generous God,
we pray for rich countries with a surplus of wealth,
    and for the poor countries in debt to them;
we pray for rich countries whose stores are overflowing,
    and for countries whose harvests have failed;
we pray for rich countries flaunting their material success,
    and for the poor who live there, forgotten or ignored.
Generous God,
help us not to pile up treasures for ourselves
while remaining paupers in your sight.   *Silence*

Generous God,
we pray for those whose wealth has given them power,
    and for those whose poverty has made them powerless;
we pray for those whose lives are given to making money,
    and for those who can barely afford to live;
we pray for the successful, the popular, the talented,
    and for those who are given little respect.
Generous God,
help us not to pile up treasures for ourselves
while remaining paupers in your sight.   *Silence*

Generous God,
we pray for your church with its many possessions,
    and for your people who live in poverty;
we pray for your church, entrusted with the gospel,
    and for those crying out for love and hope;
we pray for your church, filled with your Holy Spirit,
    and for those who long for guidance and peace.
Generous God,
help us not to pile up treasures for ourselves
while remaining paupers in your sight.   *Silence*

In the name of your Son, Jesus Christ, our Saviour,
who was rich, yet for our sakes became poor,
so that through his poverty we might become rich.   **Amen.**

Loving God,
so often your coming into our lives
takes us by surprise,
finds us unprepared.
We expect to find you in church
blessing our offering of money;
we do not expect to find you
begging from us on the streets.
We expect to meet you
in bread and wine;
we do not expect to meet you
in the eyes of a starving child.
We expect to find you
in the emotion of prayer and praise;
we do not expect to find you
in the dull pains of everyday living.

Loving God,
we pray for your church,
that we may be a people of faith,
ready to respond to your call.
We pray for the church's work in . . .
We pray for the world,
where faith in you is sorely tested,
and so many long for the dawn of a new day.
We pray for the situation in . . .
We pray for humankind,
that hope might come to those who suffer,
and courage to those who are afraid.
We pray for . . .

Loving God,
fill us with your Holy Spirit,
that we may hold ourselves in readiness
for the coming into our lives of Jesus Christ,
at the time least expected.

In his name we pray.   **Amen.**

Creator God, your world longs to live in peace.
We pray for your healing peace
   for countries at war with one another . . .
   for communities where there is conflict . . .
   for the victims of past and present wars . . .
Your world longs to live in peace,
   but not peace at any price.
We pray for those who stir up dissension
   by campaigning for justice;
   by championing the poor and oppressed;
   by challenging the wealthy and powerful.
In your love and mercy: **hear our prayer.**

Saviour God, humanity longs to live in peace.
We pray for your healing peace
   for those racked by guilt or regret;
   for those caught up in turbulent relationships;
   for those burdened by illness or sorrow.
Humanity longs to live in peace,
   but not peace at any price.
We pray for those who stir up dissension
   by questioning the ways of society;
   by being open and honest;
   by searching for the truth.
In your love and mercy: **hear our prayer.**

Spirit of God, your church longs to live in peace.
We pray for your healing peace
   between denominatons;
   within individual churches;
   in our own hearts.
Your church longs to live in peace,
   but not peace at any price.
We pray for those who stir up dissension
   disturbing us with new visions and ideas;
   criticising our apathy and complacency;
   provoking us to think afresh about our calling.
In your love and mercy: **hear our prayer.**　**Amen.**

Loving God, on this holy day
we pray for freedom
for the bowed down people of your world:
  freedom from warfare
  we pray for . . .
  freedom from hunger
  we pray for . . .
  freedom from injustice
  we pray for . . .
Lay your hands upon our lives:
and loose us from our bonds.

Loving God, on this holy day
we pray for freedom
for those bowed down by suffering:
  freedom from illness
  we pray for . . .
  freedom from anxiety
  we pray for . . .
  freedom from the anguish of loss
  we pray for . . .
Lay your hands upon our lives:
and loose us from our bonds.

Loving God, on this holy day
we pray for freedom
for those who live bowed down
under the weight of distorted religion:
  freedom from fear;
  freedom from guilt;
  freedom from complacency.
Lay your hands upon our lives:
and loose us from our bonds.

In the name of him who delights us
by his acts of saving love for humankind,
Jesus Christ, your Son, our Lord.   **Amen.**

Loving God, gracious host,
you invite humankind
to partake of the banquet of life.

We pray for the guests with wealth and power
who have secured for themselves
places of honour in our world.
Open their eyes to see the faces
of your other guests.
Open their ears to hear their requests.
Open their hands to give.

We pray for the followers of Christ,
that we might come to your table
eagerly and in humility.
May we be truly thankful
for your many gifts to us.
May we serve one another
with sensitivity and love.
May we give of what we have
without expecting any return.

We pray for those finding it difficult
to enjoy the riches of the banquet:
those who are ill . . .
those who are sorrowful . . .
those who have passed up the invitation.
Gracious host,
give them what they need to sustain them.
Give them healing and hope, comfort and love,
that they may feed on you in their hearts.

Loving God, gracious host,
may we partake of the heavenly banquet
you have prepared for all humankind.

In the name of him who came to invite us to the feast,
Jesus Christ, your Son, our Saviour.   **Amen.**

God of wisdom and generosity,
   open our eyes to see the cost
               of the things we pray for;
   and open our hearts to make us willing
               to pay that cost.

We pray for the homeless and hungry, for . . .
Loving God, inspire us to sacrificial giving,
   that they may be sheltered and fed.
We pray for the destitute and exploited, for . . .
Loving God, inspire us to seek and support fair trade,
   that they may be given just reward for their work.

We pray for those who are ill, anxious or sorrowful, for . . .
Loving God, help us to be prepared to share their pain,
   that through us they may know your loving, healing presence.
We pray for the lonely, unloved or despairing, for . . .
Loving God, help us to be prepared to befriend them,
   that through us they might experience your arms around them.

Fill us with your Holy Spirit, so that:
   when we pray for forgiveness
   we may be ready to forgive;
   when we pray to know your saving love
   we may be ready to take up our cross;
   when we pray for eternal life
   we may be ready to give our lives to you.

God of wisdom and generosity,
   open our eyes to see the cost
               of the things we pray for;
   and open our hearts to make us willing
               to pay that cost.

In the name of your Son, Jesus Christ,
who laid down his life for his friends.   **Amen.**

Hear the voices of the lost:

'I no longer feel at home in my world. I am lost because I have lost everything. The war has deprived me of home, land, family and friends.'

God, you search for your lost children and rescue them;
we pray for those caught up on the rolling tides of warfare, famine
or natural disaster. We pray for . . .
In your love and mercy: **hear our prayer.**

'I do not know what I should or can do. I feel lost because I have lost all sense of direction in my life. My illness has robbed me of self-determination.'

God, you heal your lost children and guide them;
we pray for those whose journey of life
is passing through a fog of illness or sorrow, for . . .
In your love and mercy: **hear our prayer.**

'I feel cut off from other people and from God. I am lost because of the terrible things I have done. My guilt and self-loathing have driven a wedge between me and life.'

God, you call to your lost children and forgive them;
we pray for those who despair of finding their way
to forgiveness and to love, peace and joy.
In your love and mercy: **hear our prayer.**

When we are lost, loving Shepherd,
search for us, rescue us.
Heal our self-inflicted wounds
and the hurts that life brings.
Guide us onwards, calling us by name,
forgiving us when we stray.
Lift us up, and bring us safely home.

In Jesus' name.   **Amen.**

Loving God,
we pray for those entrusted with much money,
asking that they might use it to enrich the lives of others.
We remember the politicians
  whose economic decisions affect both rich and poor.
We remember the heads of industry and business,
  as they balance the needs and demands
    of workers, customers and shareholders.
We remember the wealthy
  in peril from the many temptations that money brings;
and we pray:
Your kingdom come: **your will be done.**

Loving God,
we pray for those who receive little money,
asking that their poverty might not diminish their lives.
We remember the destitute
  in their daily struggle to meet their children's needs.
We remember the unemployed
  and all those who feel undervalued by society.
We remember those with only just enough money,
  who feel deprived in comparison with those around them;
and we pray:
Your kingdom come: **your will be done.**

Loving God,
we pray for ourselves, asking that you will guide us
in the ways in which we think about and use our money.
Help us to be good stewards
of all that you have given us;
may we be willing to share
  all that we have and all that we are
  with the needy world around us;
may we be willing to share the love of Jesus,
  who came to preach good news to the poor.
We pray:
Your kingdom come: **your will be done.**
In Christ's name.   **Amen.**

'The love of money is the root of all evil.'

Generous God,
    all around us we see the evidence
    of lives ruined by the love of money.
We see unhappy people
    who have put all their efforts into getting rich,
    but are discontented and unfulfilled.
We see disappointed people
    who have gambled away what they had
    in the hope of getting more.
We see lonely people
    who have sacrificed relationships
    in the pursuit of wealth.
We pray for them, asking that they might turn to you
and discover the lasting treasure of your love.
Help them to grasp the Life that is life indeed.
In your love and mercy: **hear our prayer.**

Generous God,
    all around us we see the evidence
    of lives ruined by the greed of others.
We see poor and hungry people
    whose labour has been exploited
    by wealthy employers and nations.
We see deprived children
    neglected by parents working long hours
    to maintain a certain lifestyle.
We see suffering people
    in societies where those who have
    are unwilling to share with those who have not.
We pray for them, asking that you might restore their lives through
the concern and generosity of your people.
Help them to grasp the Life that is life indeed.
In your love and mercy: **hear our prayer.**

In the name of Jesus Christ,
our Lord, our Life, our Treasure.   **Amen.**

Faithful God,
    we pray for those of your people
    who are hanging on to faith in you
    by their fingertips,
    while the everyday securities of life
    collapse around them.
We pray: for those, like the people of Judah,
           who are strangers and exiles far from home;
           for those who are exiled from normality
           by illness, anxiety, or bereavement;
           for those estranged from people they love
           by the breakdown of relationships of trust.
Silence
With the disciples, we say to the Lord: **'Increase our faith.'**

Faithful God,
    we pray for those of your people
    whose faith is weakening and dying,
    tested beyond endurance
    by the pain of living.
We pray: for those who, like the early Christians
           are persecuted and penalized for their beliefs;
           for those whose belief in the power of love has been
           shattered by the suffering of an innocent loved one;
           for those who have sought you in the church
           but found little wholeness there.
Silence
With the disciples, we say to the Lord: **'Increase our faith.'**

Faithful God,
    we pray for ourselves
    for the times when our faith remains a duty
    but has lost its delight.
We pray for the gift of your life-giving Spirit.   *Silence*
With the disciples, we say to the Lord: **'Increase our faith'**
that we may serve you forever, in Jesus' name.   **Amen.**

*'Jesus was met by ten men with leprosy. They . . . called out to him,
"Jesus, Master, take pity on us."'*

Healer and Saviour,
we are the ones who call out to you for help.
We are the unclean,
whose dis-ease with ourselves, one another, and you
needs your cure.
We pray that you will touch:
   those sick in body, mind or spirit;
   the sorrowful and anxious;
   the guilt-ridden and depressed;
and soothe their pain,
cleansing and restoring them.

*'. . . they were made clean. One of them . . . turned back, with shouts
of praise to God. He threw himself at Jesus's feet and thanked him.'*

Healer and Saviour,
help us to be the ones who turn back to you,
to be a thankful people
whose own healing and forgiveness
shows itself in faith and love.
We pray that you will touch your church:
   uniting us in praise and service;
   filling us with enthusiasm and joy;
   increasing and confirming our faith in you;
that through us the world may come to Christ,
to be cleansed and restored.

*'And Jesus said to the man, "Stand up and go on your way; your
faith has cured you."'*

Thanks be to you, our God,
for your gracious, saving love, known in Jesus Christ,
that lifts us up, sets us right,
and sends us on our way. **Amen.**

God of life and love without limit,
we pray for those
who long to see the world a better place,
but have grown cynical,
and feel defeated.
We remember:
    those who campaign for justice and human rights;
    those who work with the victims of disaster or war;
    those who enter politics in answer to your call;
and we ask you:
help us to keep on praying: **and never lose heart.**

God of life and love without limit,
we pray for those
who long for a better quality of life
but whose hopes have been so often dashed
that they despair.
We remember:
    those with long-term illnesses;
    those existing in poverty;
    those unable to make loving relationships;
and we ask you:
help us to keep on praying: **and never lose heart.**

God of life and love without limit,
we pray for those
who long to share the good news of Jesus Christ
but have met with little response,
and feel discouraged.
We remember:
    the missionary work of this congregation;
    our nurture and teaching of the young;
    our individual witness and service;
and we ask you:
help us to keep on praying: **and never lose heart.**

In the name of Jesus Christ, your Son, our Saviour,
who remained faithful and obedient to the end.   **Amen.**

Living God,
like water poured on to thirsty ground,
your love is poured into our lives;
a trickle, a stream, a mighty river,
satisfying, renewing, refreshing us.

Living God,
give us open hearts to receive your love.
We pray for those whose hearts are closed to you,
   by pride,
      fear or
      selfishness,
that they might let you
into their lives.
In your love and mercy: **hear our prayer.**

Living God,
give us open minds to know your love.
We pray for those whose minds are closed to you,
   by ignorance,
      cynicism or
      apathy,
that they might recognize you
in their lives.
In your love and mercy: **hear our prayer.**

Living God,
give us open hands to share your love.
We pray for those who hold out their hands to us,
   for the poor
      the loveless and
      those in pain,
that we might pour your love
into their lives.
In your love and mercy: **hear our prayer.**

In the name of Jesus Christ your Son,
the water of life that never runs dry. **Amen.**

'Zacchaeus . . . was eager to see what Jesus looked like; but, being a little man, he could not see him for the crowd.'

So much can get in the way of people seeing and knowing you, loving God.
Sometimes it is the crowd of believers, your church, with all our faults and failings. Sometimes the distractions of everyday life can smother efforts to find you.
God of our salvation, help us, as disciples of Jesus Christ, to clear the way for others to see him.

'Jesus . . . said, "Zacchaeus, be quick and come down, for I must stay in your house today."'

Jesus was quick to see Zacchaeus and his need and went out of his way to offer friendship and love.
God of our salvation, help us, as disciples of Jesus Christ, to see the needs of others, and to go out of our way to meet them: to give comfort to the suffering, companionship to the lonely and aid to the poor.

'Zacchaeus . . . said to the Lord, "Here and now, sir, I give half my possessions to charity; and if I have defrauded anyone, I will repay him four times over."'

Faith in you, loving God, turns our lives around.
We see everything with new eyes.
Wrongs are righted, sins forgiven.
God of our salvation, help us, as disciples of Jesus Christ, to reveal our love for you, and your saving love for all humankind, in the ways in which we live, speak and care.

In the name of Jesus Christ,
who is your beloved Son and the Son of Man
and who came to seek and to save the lost.   **Amen.**

God of the living, of renewal and change,
we pray for those who long for change:
    for the victims of injustice;
                   warfare;
                   poverty;
    for . . .
    for those enduring illness;
                   anxiety;
                   sorrow;
    for . . .
    and for those dissatisfied
    with their lives and with themselves,
    who long to be shaken up,
    made new, reborn as your children.
We pray for those who long for change.
In your love and mercy: **hear our prayer.**

God of the living, of renewal and change,
we pray for those beset by change:
    for those threatened by the breakdown of
                   their community;
                   traditional values;
                   long-held beliefs;
    for . . .
    for those facing bereavement;
                   redundancy
                   divorce;
    for . . .
    and for those without
    financial, emotional or spiritual security,
    who long for inner peace,
    for the gift of faith.
We pray for those beset by change.
In your love and mercy: **hear our prayer.**

In the name of our eternal Saviour, Jesus Christ.   **Amen.**

Creator God,
    wars between nations,
    conflicts between communities,
    earthquakes,
    famines,
    plagues;
still we hear about them every day,
and see the suffering that they bring.
Today we pray for . . .
Loving God, we long for an end to such destruction.
Your kingdom come: **your will be done.**

Saviour God,
    persecution,
    martyrdom,
    fear,
    pain,
    death;
still your children are suffering
in body, mind and spirit.
Today we pray for . . .
Loving God, we long for an end to such darkness.
Your kingdom come: **your will be done.**

Spirit of God,
    disunity,
    apathy,
    hypocrisy,
    faithlessness,
    lack of love;
still your temple is being torn down stone by stone,
your church attacked from within and without.
Today we pray for . . .
Loving God, we long for an end to such desecration.
Your kingdom come: **your will be done.**

In the name of Jesus Christ, who stood firm until the end,
to win life for all humankind.   **Amen.**

'Father, forgive them; they do not know what they are doing.'
Father, forgive us as we blunder on in ignorance,
destroying what is good:
   polluting the earth;
   exploiting the labour of the poor;
   consuming more than we need;
   hurting those around us.
Open the eyes of the people of your world,
that they may see and know what they are doing,
and turn back to you.
In your love and mercy: **hear our prayer.**

'Are you not the Messiah? Save yourself and us.'
Saviour, help us in times of suffering:
                  of illness and pain;
                  of bereavement and sorrow;
                  of anxiety and despair;
                  of guilt and regret.
We pray for . . .
asking that you will be with all those who suffer,
healing, strengthening and comforting them,
and giving them hope.
In your love and mercy: **hear our prayer.**

'Truly, I tell you; today you will be with me in Paradise.'
God with us, we ask above all for your presence,
                  your love,
                  your peace,
                  your strength,
                  your joy.
May our lives, and the life of the world,
be renewed and transformed
by trust in your unfailing care.
In your love and mercy: **hear our prayer.**

In the name of Jesus Christ, through whom you chose to reconcile all
things to yourself.   **Amen.**

Special Days

Christmas Day – Set I readings

A baby, born in the night
to a young mother, wearied by journeying.
Loving God, we pray for all those wearied by their journey to this
    Christmas Day:
        the exhausted and stressed . . .
        the anxious and afraid . . .
        those who live with conflict . . .
        those who live with need . . .
        those weighed down by illness . . .
        those heavy with sorrow or grief . . .
Light of Christ: **dawn in our darkness.**

A baby, born in the night
to an anxious couple, far from home.
Loving God, we pray for all those who feel far from their homes
    this Christmas Day:
        the refugees from war or persecution . . .
        the incomers in a strange land . . .
        those working away from home . . .
        those divided from their families by disagreement . . .
        those who are lonely even amongst others . . .
        those who are lonely because they are alone . . .
Light of Christ: **dawn in our darkness.**

A baby, born in the night
to all humankind, to bring us joy.
Loving God, we pray for ourselves, the family of Christ, this
    Christmas Day:
        the sisters and brothers here with us now . . .
        the extended family throughout the world . . .
        those working amongst the needy . . .
        those announcing the Good News . . .
        those finding faith hard . . .
        those whose memory we cherish . . .
Light of Christ: **dawn in our darkness.**

We pray in the name of him who has increased our joy and given us
great gladness, Jesus Christ, God with us.   **Amen.**

Christmas Day – Set II readings

Glory to you, generous Creator,
who so loved your world
that you sent your Son
to be born as Messiah to us,
to bring us peace.
This Christmas day
we ask for your special gifts for the world:
    for justice . . .   *Silence*
    for plenty . . .   *Silence*
    for freedom . . .   *Silence*
    for peace . . .   *Silence*

Glory to you, humble Saviour,
who so loved humankind
that you gave yourself to us,
to be born as one of us,
to bring us salvation.
This Christmas day
we ask for your special gifts for humankind:
    for forgiveness . . .   *Silence*
    for healing . . .   *Silence*
    for victory over death . . .   *Silence*
    for life in all its fullness . . .   *Silence*

Glory to you, life-giving Spirit,
who so loves us
that you choose to lavish yourself upon us,
to live in our hearts,
to bring us love.
This Christmas day
we ask for your special gifts:
    for faith . . .   *Silence*
    for comfort . . .   *Silence*
    for fellowship . . .   *Silence*
    for joy . . .   *Silence*

Glory to you our God, Creator, Saviour, Spirit, for you give yourself
as the answer to our prayers.   **Amen.**

Christmas Day – Set III readings

*'The light shines in the darkness
and the darkness has never mastered it.'*

God, who called creation into being,
we pray for light for the dark places of your world:
    where there is conflict and war,
      let there be peace;
    where there is injustice and discrimination,
      let there be justice;
    where there is poverty and hunger,
      let there be plenty;
    where there is oppression and exploitation,
      let there be freedom.
Come, light of God: **shine in our darkness.**

God, who made your home among us,
we pray for light for dark lives:
    where there is illness or infirmity,
      let there be healing;
    where there is anxiety or depression,
      let there be joy;
    where there is sorrow or grief,
      let there be comfort;
    where there is guilt or hatred,
      let there be forgiveness.
Come, light of God: **shine in our darkness.**

God, who gives new life to your children,
we pray for light for our dark days:
    in times of doubt or despair,
      let there be new insights of faith;
    in times of suffering for love's sake,
      let there be fresh courage;
    in times of division or disagreement,
      let there be an arresting call for unity;
    in times of apathy and complacency,
      let there be a vision for the future.
Come, light of God: **shine in our darkness.**   **Amen.**

Watchnight

We see in the New Year. We watch together.
We watch for the coming of Christ.

Creator God, we watch for your coming
   into the life of the world you have made.
We watch for a new heaven and a new earth.
Come, Lord, come,
as freedom to the oppressed;
   justice to the exploited;
   food to those who hunger.
We are ready and waiting.
Come, loving God: **and renew us.**

Saviour God, we watch for your coming
   into the lives of humankind.
We watch for the wiping away of tears.
Come, Lord, come,
as healing to the sick;
   forgiveness to the sinful;
   comfort to those who mourn.
We are ready and waiting.
Come, loving God: **and renew us.**

Spirit of God, we watch for your coming
   into our lives.
We watch for the renewal of your people.
Come, Lord, come,
as love to bind us together;
   hope to give us vision and courage;
   enthusiasm to fire our witness to you.
We are ready and waiting.
Come, loving God: **and renew us.**

On the threshold of this New Year,
knock on the door of our lives, loving God,
for we are ready to open to you,
to walk with you the way of self-giving love
all the days that are to come, in Jesus' name.   **Amen.**

The Epiphany

God of glory, we lay the gold of the world
at the feet of the Christ-child
offering it for transformation
   from the gold amassed by selfish greed
     into the gold used with caring generosity;
   from the gold wielded as an instrument of power
     into the gold given to the victims of powerlessness.
We pray for those who have wealth and power . . .   *Silence*
    and for the poor and powerless . . .   *Silence*
God of glory, we lay our wealth and prayers
at the feet of the Christ-child.
Jesus, Son of God: **Accept our offerings of love.**

God of glory, we lay the incense of worship
at the feet of the Christ-child
offering it for transformation
   from the worship that gives us good feelings
     into the worship that encourages us to seek goodness;
   from worship performed out of duty
     into worship expressing loving delight.
We pray for the worship life of the church . . .   *Silence*
    and for the worship of our everyday lives . . .   *Silence*
God of glory, we lay our worship and prayers
at the feet of the Christ-child.
Jesus, Son of God: **Accept our offerings of love.**

God of glory, we lay the myrrh of suffering
at the feet of the Christ-child
offering it for transformation
   from suffering that leads to bitterness and despair
     into suffering that finds comfort and hope;
   from suffering that seems meaningless and futile
     into suffering that reveals and redeems.
We pray for those suffering in any way . . .   *Silence*
  and for those who suffer with them . . .   *Silence*
God of glory, we lay our suffering and prayers
at the feet of the Christ-child.
Jesus, Son of God: **Accept our offerings of love.**   **Amen.**

Ash Wednesday

Gracious God,
we would grieve with you over the sins of your world:
   the sin of warfare
      that leaves a young, strong man
      with no sight and no hope; *Silence*
   the sin of injustice
      that leaves a dissident woman in prison
      tortured, degraded and betrayed; *Silence*
   the sin of greed
      that leaves a swollen-bellied child
      weakly wailing with hunger. *Silence*
Gracious God,
we would grieve with your over the sins of our world.
We pray for a true repentance,
         a turning of hearts and minds and lives.
God, create a pure heart for us:
   give us a new and steadfast spirit.

Gracious God,
we would grieve with you over the sins of humankind:
   the sin of selfishness
      that leaves us seeing only our own needs,
      blinding us to the needs of others; *Silence*
   the sin of fear
      that imprisons, limits and alienate us
      diminishing our humanity and our loving; *Silence*
   the sin of materialism
      that worships the trivial and the transient
      and leaves us unsatisfied and despairing. *Silence*
Gracious God,
we would grieve with your over the sins of humankind.
We pray for a true repentance,
         a turning of hearts and minds and lives.
God, create a pure heart for us:
   give us a new and steadfast spirit.

In the name of Jesus Christ, who came to call sinners to repentance
and to lead us into the kingdom of God. **Amen.**

Mothering Sunday – Year B readings

*'I hold my baby in my arms. She is so small, so helpless, so
demanding. Motherhood moves, excites, and scares me.'*
We pray for those who have recently become parents.
We think of those welcoming a wanted child and those burdened by
the birth; those with a healthy, strong child and those whose child is
ill or has disabilities; those equipped by their childhood to be loving
and supportive, and those who were abused or neglected and will
have to struggle with themselves. We ask that their homes might be
places of love, joy and respect, where children and adults grow
together in wisdom and understanding. We pray for those who long
for children but have not yet realized their dream of holding their
child in their arms. We ask that your love might soothe the ache of
emptiness in their lives.
Mothering God: **hear our prayer.**

*'I hold my child in my arms. He is malnourished and sick.
I can do nothing for him. O God, help me.'*
We pray for those watching as their children suffer.
We think of those whose children are ill, or injured; those who have
a struggle to feed their children, and those who have a struggle to
give their children the love they crave; those whose children are
lonely or bullied and of those who themselves abuse their family. We
ask, merciful God, that they might find help, comfort and support in
the knowledge and experience of your parental love for them.
Mothering God: **hear our prayer.**

*'I can no longer hold my daughter in my arms. I am too old, too
weak. I need her more than she needs me.'*
We pray for those who are dependent on their children, and for
children who have to take care of their parents. We think of parents
frail in body or mind, or chronically sick. We ask that you will give
both carer and cared for the love, strength and patience that they
need.
Mothering God: **hear our prayer.**

In the name of Jesus, son of Mary.　　**Amen.**

Good Friday

Betrayed. The Son of Man betrayed.
Betrayed by Judas. Betrayed by the crowd.
And denied by Peter, his most ardent friend.
Faithful God, we pray for those suffering from a sense of betrayal:
betrayed by governments who peddle false promises; betrayed by
those they have trusted; betrayed by those they love; betrayed by
their own weakness; betrayed by a church that has failed them.
Silence

Interrogated. The Son of Man interrogated.
Interrogated by Annas, Caiaphas and Pilate.
And jeered at by the crowd.
Truthful God, we pray for those who have come to a questioning
time in their lives: struggling to discover who you are, the right way
they should go, the true priorities for life; and for those whose beliefs
and principles are ridiculed; for those who are doubt-ridden, anxious
and perplexed. *Silence*

Tortured. The Son of Man tortured.
Flogged and forced to wear a crown of thorns.
Carrying the heavy cross. And hung upon it.
Suffering God, we pray for those leading a tortured existence: the ill
in chronic pain or with life-limiting weakness; the mentally disturbed
and confused; the depressed living with inner darkness; and those
bereaved or consumed with sorrow or fear. *Silence*

Killed. The Son of Man killed.
His offered life taken away
by government, established religion, the people themselves.
Dying God, we pray for those who are dying, those who watch over
them, those who love them, those who tend them.
We thank you for those who have died in the faith. *Silence*
Living God, we pray for ourselves, that we might give our lives to
you and your way of self-giving love and so find new and everlasting
life in Christ. *Silence*
In the name of our crucified King. **Amen.**

Ascension Day

Freed from the constraints of time and space,
of human body and human needs,
Christ lives with us now,
the Risen, Ascended Lord of all.

Let us pray for those who need to know the liberating presence of
God in their lives.

God of every time and place,
we pray for all who work for freedom:
   those who face up to the might of repressive
   governments . . . *Silence*
   those promoting fair trade between rich and poor
   countries . . . *Silence*
   those providing education and healthcare for the
   needy . . . *Silence*
   those preaching the gospel of forgiveness and new life
   . . . *Silence*
Our prayers are heard: **Thanks be to God.**

God of the here and now,
we pray for all who seek release:
   those whose lives are limited by illness . . . *Silence*
   those who find life unbearable . . . *Silence*
   those burdened with sorrow or anxiety . . . *Silence*
   those imprisoned by fear or guilt . . . *Silence*
Our prayers are heard: **Thanks be to God.**

God within us and around us
we pray for the gift of your Holy Spirit:
   to break down the barriers between us . . . *Silence*
   to release us from our fears . . . *Silence*
   to free us to be ourselves in you . . . *Silence*
   to empower us with your love . . . *Silence*
Our prayers are heard: **Thanks be to God.**

Be with us, loving God, in all the ups and downs of our lives,
now and for evermore, in Jesus' name. **Amen.**

Conversion of John and Charles Wesley – 24/5

Loving God, we pray for the warming of hearts;
   for the salvation of all humankind;
   for a deeper relationship of faith with you.

'Your love is unfailing and great is your power to deliver.'
We pray for those with power in your world,
that in the exercise of that power
   they may be ruled not only by their heads,
   but by loving hearts.
We ask that wisdom may be informed by compassion;
              justice be tempered by mercy;
              policies be determined by human need.
Out of the depths we call to you: **hear our cry.**

'He alone will set Israel free. . .'
We pray for those who want to be released,
saved from lives imprisoned
   by hunger and poverty, illness and sorrow;
   by sin and guilt, anxiety and fear.
We ask that your love might reach out and touch them,
   loosing their chains,
   setting them free.
Out of the depths we call to you: **hear our cry.**

'I wait for the Lord with longing . . .'
We pray for those who, like John and Charles Wesley,
long for a deeper relationship of faith with you;
   for those seeking you in their lives and in the church,
   but assailed by doubts and afraid of commitment.
We pray for ourselves,
for members of the Methodist Church throughout the world,
for all Christians, asking that we may know
   your peace, strengthening our trust in you;
   your love, building us up and binding us together;
   your hope, calling us on to new ways of serving you.
Out of the depths we call to you: **hear our cry.**
In the name of him to whom we now belong,
Jesus Christ, our glorious Saviour.   **Amen.**

Harvest Festival

Creator God, we pray for the world you have given us.
We thank you for:
    the soil in which we plant our seeds;
    the pasture on which we graze our animals;
    the natural and mineral resources that feed and fuel our
       industries;
    the seas and rivers which we fish.
We ask that you will help us:
    to treat your world with respect;
    to observe the rhythms and balance of nature;
    to conserve the earth's riches and resources
       for generations to come.
God of the harvest: **hear our prayer.**

Saviour God, we pray for needy humankind;
for those without a harvest because:
    hunger drove them to eat their seed corn;
    their land is ravished by drought, flood or war;
    their animals are diseased and dying;
    their waters have been over-fished;
    their natural resources are running out.
We ask that you will help us to help them;
    and to see your world as one world,
    acknowledging one another's needs and rights.
God of the harvest: **hear our prayer.**

Life-giving Spirit, we pray for your church,
that we might harvest the fruit
of your love sown in our hearts,
the fruit of faith, hope and love, joy and peace.
We ask that you will help us feed hungry souls
with the Good News of Jesus, the Bread of Life.
God of the harvest: **hear our prayer.**

In the name of Jesus Christ,
who came to reap the harvest of salvation.　　**Amen.**

All Saints' Day — Year B readings

'The souls of the just are in God's hands.'
God of life and death,
the Alpha and the Omega, the beginning and the end,
we remember before you, with thanks, the lives of those Christians
who have gone before us: the great leaders and thinkers; those who
died for their faith; those whose goodness transformed all they
touched and those we have known and loved, who have had great
influence on our Christian lives. Give us the grace to follow their
example as we continue their work for the coming of your kingdom.

'He shall wipe every tear from their eyes.'
God of life and death,
the Alpha and the Omega, the beginning and the end,
we remember before you those from this Christian community who
have recently died . . . giving thanks for their lives and example and
for all that they have meant to us. We pray for those who grieve for
them, for . . . We pray, too, for members of the church, both here and
throughout the world who are suffering or sorrowful: for the hungry,
the sick, the victims of violence and persecution. Give them the
comfort of your loving presence.

'I am making all things new.'
God of life and death,
the Alpha and the Omega, the beginning and the end,
we remember before you the newest generation of your saints, and
pray for the future of the church. We pray for those recently baptized
and welcomed into the membership of the church . . . and for all
responsible for the Christian nurture of the young. Give us your Holy
Spirit that we may be faithful to you and your way of love through
every future change and challenge and bring us with all your saints
into your kingdom of everlasting life.

In the name of Jesus Christ,
the Lord and Saviour of us all.   **Amen.**

Church Anniversary

Loving God, we pray for this church, asking
that your Holy Spirit may inspire our worship
   and lead us into deeper fellowship;
that we may pass on the teaching of our faith
   and our traditions of service to new generations;
that within our fellowship there may be found
   comfort for the sorrowful, strength for the anxious,
   compassion for those who are ill,
   and concern and love for all.
We pray for the other churches in this area,
   for the breaking down of barriers between believers,
that in unity we may strive to serve this community,
   with commitment, vision and enthusiasm.
This is our prayer: **Help us to know and to do your will.**

Loving God, we pray for those with positions of
responsiblity within this church:
   for our minister, for preachers and teachers;
   for stewards, treasurers, pastoral visitors;
   for youth workers and group leaders, for . . .
asking that they may find the resources of faith
   to equip them for their tasks,
and that they may fulfill their calling eagerly,
   conscientiously and with imagination.
This is our prayer: **Help us to know and to do your will.**

Loving God, we pray for those of our church family
who are in any kind of trouble or need:
   for those who are ill . . .
   for those who are anxious . . .
   for those who have been bereaved . . .
May they be upheld by your presence and our prayers.
We remember with love those no longer able to get to church . . .
those who have moved away . . . those who have died . . .
This is our prayer: **Help us to know and to do your will.**

In the name of Christ, our cornerstone.   **Amen.**

Remembrance Sunday

On this Remembrance Sunday,
we remember past wars:
those who fought in them;
those who lived through them;
those who died in them.
Silence

We pray for the victims of past wars,
remembering before you, loving God,
those who died in battle,
   or from the consequences of injury or disease,
and those who mourned or still mourn them.
We remember those permanently maimed or disabled,
and those psychologically scarred or disturbed.
We pray for an end to the suffering of war.
Silence

We pray for the victims of current conflicts,
remembering before you, loving God,
children trained to hate and fight,
families turned into homeless refugees,
and lands laid waste and made barren.
We remember those blinded and crippled
and those driven insane by nightmare experiences.
We pray for an end to the destructive hatred of war.
Silence

We pray for the peace of the world
remembering before you, loving God,
areas where there is armed conflict . . .
and all those who are working for peace.
We remember that you have called us to strive together
for the coming of your kingdom of love and peace.
We pray that you will equip us for the task
with the faith that knows
that nothing can separate us from the love of Christ.

In the name of Jesus, Prince of Peace.   **Amen.**

Index of Themes